We have known Lee  ars now. They have made ors and church leaders of the principles of healing and deliverance so clearly explained in this book. The demonstrations of the healing models and prayer for the sick have resulted in many remarkable testimonies in India. Being an engineer, Lee has explained healing and deliverance in a simple and analytical manner. This information can easily be used as a guide or reference book.

ABRAHAM AND SHEILA SEKHAR
Chairpersons of Global Mercy Foundation of India, Overseers of Spirit Filled Churches of India (a network of over 3,000 churches)

Lee and Doris Harms have been members of my congregation for fourteen years. I have watched them minister to the sick and demonized, and it is very evident that this takes place out of their love for Jesus. They have also trained many to "lay hands on the sick (and see them) recover." Their practical approach has helped equip many to take up this mandate and do so in an effective manner.

ALAN KOCH
Senior Pastor, Christ Triumphant Church, Lee's Summit, MO

The healing ministry of Jesus has sometimes been maligned and rejected because of the excesses of a few within the body of Christ. In a way that is biblical, genuine, and unpretentious, Lee and Doris show us how to participate in this vital dimension of living as a disciple of Jesus Christ. As one who has personal experience with their ministry in a variety of settings, I heartily recommend them and their ministry. Their story will increase your faith.

PASTOR BRUCE KOTILA
Thanksgiving! Lutheran Church, Bellevue, NE

HEALING AND DELIVERANCE
FUNDAMENTALS

LEE HARMS

Healing and Deliverance Foundations
Copyright 2014 by Leland Harms
All rights reserved.

ISBN: 978-0-9833152-9-2

King of Glory Ministries International Publications 2014
King of Glory Ministries International
PO Box 903, Moravian Falls, NC 28654
336-818-1210 or 828-320-3502
www.kingofgloryministries.org

All Rights Reserved. No part of this book may be reproduced or transmitted in any form or by any means—electronic or mechanical, including photocopying, recording, or by any information storage and retrieval system—without written permission from the authors except as provided by the copyright laws of the United States of America. Unauthorized reproduction is a violation of federal as well as spiritual laws.

Unless otherwise noted, all scripture quotations are from the New American Standard Bible. Copyright © 1960, 1962, 1963, 1968, 1971, 1972, 1973, 1975, 1977 by the Lockman Foundation. Used by permission. (www.Lockman.org).

Scripture quotations marked KJV are from the King James Version of the Bible.

Cover design and layout by projectluz.com
Printed in the United States of America

TABLE OF CONTENTS

Acknowledgments vii

Preface ix

PART 1: PHYSICAL HEALING

CHAPTER 1
Knowing God's Will in Healing 1

CHAPTER 2
The Healing Word and the Authority to Heal the Sick 19

CHAPTER 3
The Anointing for Healing 31

CHAPTER 4
Using the Word of Knowledge in Healing 39

CHAPTER 5
Healing Models 49

CHAPTER 6
Healing in the Glory 63

CHAPTER 7
Ministering to the Critically Ill 67

CHAPTER 8
What to Do when Healing Doesn't Come 81

PART 2: DELIVERANCE

CHAPTER 9
Healing the Demonized 89

CHAPTER 10
Some Characteristics of Demons 97

CHAPTER 11
A Typical Deliverance Session 101

CHAPTER 12
Ministering Deliverance to Children 115

CHAPTER 13
Cleansing of Places 123

About the Author 129

Acknowledgments

This book would never have been written or published without the prompting of the Lord. He has been faithful to send His prophetic servants to remind me that I have a book to write, so it is with mostly a sense of obedience that these pages are now before you. I am thankful to the obedient servants of Jesus who have reminded me to put these thoughts on paper.

This material has been tested during classroom sessions with students of the former Grace Training Center, which was a part of Metro Christian Fellowship of Kansas City; as well as in training sessions for our healing rooms, various seminars, and teaching times. I am grateful to all who participated in these sessions as they put forth many thought provoking questions which helped solidify my own thoughts regarding healing and deliverance.

Thank You, precious Holy Spirit, for all the guidance, revelation, and power we have seen so often as we ministered to the ones You love. You are truly the One who leads us into all truth. I'd also like to recognize the impact of Charles and Frances Hunter on my life, both who are now enjoying the eternal fruits of their labors and relationship with the Lord. Their example, perseverance, faith in the Lord, teaching, and encouragement impacted us greatly. So many others have encouraged us and given us opportunities to minister along the way; Dr. James Goll, Mike Bickle, Jill Austin, Cal Pierce, and Pastors Alan and Carol Koch, to mention a few.

I would be remiss if I did not express my appreciation to Doris, my helpmate of over fifty years. She has been my partner as we learned the "ins and outs" of the healing and deliverance ministry. Thanks, Doris, for hanging in there when the going wasn't easy, for believing in me and what the Lord was doing with us, and for sharing your thoughts and insights with me.

Preface

One of my favorite authors, Jamie Buckingham, said he'd like to write a book without a preface sometime because nobody read it anyway. But just in case somebody does read this, I'll take the opportunity to say a couple of things.

First, the main purpose of writing this book is to encourage all the "little folks" to keep on doing what they think the Lord has asked them to do. Most of God's people will never have a public ministry, speak from a pulpit, or have their name in print, etc.; yet, the many little things done daily by the millions of nameless Christians make up the real expression of Christianity on the earth. When we reach out to our sick neighbor with a meal, when we provide gasoline for a struggling soul, when we pray for that sick co-worker; the name of the Lord is lifted up and He is blessed by our heart attitude as well as our deeds.

Doris and I feel like we're one of you, one of the "little folks." We've never planted a church, lived from the tithe, or had much public recognition. We earned our living just like you, going to work each day. Yet, we've prayed and ministered to literally thousands of people in our home or theirs, at the church, after services, and in the U.S. and overseas. We've been lost in the middle of the Czech Republic, slept on steel beds in India, and preached through a translator in New York City. We've ministered in some pretty tiny places, like the Agape Christian Center in Amidon, North Dakota, population twenty-three; and we saw some things happen there we still remember and share about. I sometimes think the Lord sends us to unpopulated areas because we don't need an offering to pay our bills. We've seen the Lord do many wonderful and exciting things, and we're expecting to see much more before we're through. I hope you do too.

Secondly, I pray that as you read these pages you will be able to capture the sense of love and awe that we have for our awesome God. Doris and I have been ministering to the sick and demonized for over thirty-five years now and still have difficulty believing that He is using us to participate in His wonderful acts of mercy and grace.

The stories in this book are all true, as they were told to us and as we recall them. Periodically as we have ministered we decided we should document some of the healings, so it would "prove God" to the skeptics; but the believers didn't need the documentation and the skeptics didn't seem to pay much attention to any documentation. So, by and large, these stories are without medical or other written documentation, but they are as true in detail as we know how to make them. We have changed some of the names to protect people from being exposed or embarrassed.

We've tried to resist only telling stories that turn out well from our perspective. When we first starting ministering to the sick, only about 10 percent seemed to improve or be healed. Our percentage is much higher than that now, but we still minister to many people without any noticeable results. Also, initially it seemed that if we would just persevere, any evil spirit we encountered would have to leave and the person could be set free. I've run into some spirits now that wouldn't leave, for whatever reason.

These "failures" have reinforced what we've known all along—it is indeed the Lord that heals and delivers; we just get to help. And frankly, in the Lord's eyes, these situations may not be logged as failures. At least we cared, we tried, and we extended love as best we knew how. We try to follow the motto that hangs in our office from 1 Corinthians 16:14: "*Let all that you do be done in love.*"

Jesus was going throughout all Galilee, teaching in their synagogues and proclaiming the gospel of the kingdom, and healing every kind of disease and every kind of sickness among the people. The news about Him spread throughout all Syria; and they brought to Him all who were ill, those suffering with various diseases and pains, demoniacs, epileptics, paralytics; and He healed them.
—Matthew 4:23-24

Jesus summoned His twelve disciples and gave them authority over unclean spirits, to cast them out, and to heal every kind of disease and every kind of sickness.
—Matthew 10:1

PART I
PHYSICAL HEALING

CHAPTER 1

Knowing God's Will in Healing

Years ago I didn't actually expect God to directly heal anyone, so I didn't ask Him to heal. Now that I know people can be healed through prayer, it opens up another arena in which to experience the goodness of God; but the inconsistencies we see regarding divine healing also makes life a little more confusing. Does God always want to heal? If He does, why isn't everybody we pray for healed? If He doesn't want everybody healed, why not? Does God make people sick? If so, why? Do I have to reach a certain level of holiness or spiritual maturity in order to be healed? If so, what about grace? These are important questions that I've struggled with and probably some of you have struggled with them too. I don't pretend to have all the answers, but I've learned some things about healing and hopefully they will help you understand a little better also.

How Do I Know That God Wants to Heal?

God's normal attitude toward us is to want us healthy in body, soul, and spirit. If we are ill, then healing is a necessary expression of His goodness toward us. Let's examine some reasons why I believe this to be true.

First of all, healing originated with God and it's His idea, not ours. In Exodus 15:26 the Lord announces that He is the Lord that heals. He calls Himself Jehovah Rapha, the Lord your Healer. Just as God is love (see

1 John 4:8, 16), God is Healer. He is perfect; He cannot change. If He changed He would become imperfect, and that is impossible. He can't quit loving you; He can't stop wanting you well. The Israelites did not beg him for healing; He just told them healing was part of what He does. This is important for us to understand. We need to realize that healing comes from the heart and character of God and it is not a response to men begging for relief from pain or disease.

Secondly, Jesus demonstrated the heart of the Father while He walked the earth; and He healed, and healed, and healed. Many places in the Scripture indicate that Jesus healed *all* that needed it (see Matthew 4:24; 8:16, for example). Jesus said that He only did what He saw the Father doing (John 5:19), so we can be assured that healing is within God's desire for us. The only time it is recorded in the Gospels that Jesus was questioned about His will to heal, He immediately responded and said: "*I am willing; be cleansed*" (Matthew 8:3).

It's apparent that Jesus normally healed all those that needed or requested healing from Him (see Matthew 4:24; 8:16; Luke 4:40; 9:11; Acts 5:16, for example) and the early church seemed to follow that pattern. Yet, when Jesus came to the pool of Bethesda (John 5:1-9), He healed only one man, although there were a multitude of sick, lame, blind, and withered around the pool. Why did Jesus heal only the one man who had been ill for thirty-eight years? Why did He not heal all the others? Recently I realized that in the years preceding Jesus' ministry and the establishing of the new covenant, the Father, in His desire to bring healing to the sick, would send an angel to stir the waters in the pool so healing could come to one individual. Jesus healed only one man at that location because it had been the Father's decision to heal only one person at a time there; and He did what He saw the Father doing in like manner (John 5:19). We don't know how often the waters in the pool were stirred. It could have been once a week, once a day, once an hour, etc. It must have been frequent enough that people were encouraged to gather there and wait for the waters to be stirred. If it only happened infrequently, they likely would not have stationed themselves there.

And what about the time Jesus was in His hometown of Nazareth where He only healed a few sick people (Mark 6:1-6)? A careful reading of this passage shows us that the town's people were offended at Jesus and likely not many presented themselves for His healing touch. They had witnessed miracles and listened to His teaching in wonder, but they did not recognize that this was not the same carpenter's son who grew up in their midst. This was the sinless Son of Man who had been empowered with the Holy Spirit of God. He was physically familiar to them but they did not understand who was in their midst to heal and set free. Their pride was offended, and it kept them from receiving what He had to give. God still deals with us this way today. If we do not want what He has to offer, He will not force it on us.

Let's look more closely at John 5:19. Jesus is speaking and says:

Truly, truly, I say to you, the Son can do nothing of Himself, **unless** *it is something He sees the Father doing; for whatever the Father does, these things the Son also does in like manner* (emphasis added).

Sometimes we have the idea that Jesus never acted on His own initiative but only acted if He had divine supernatural revelation that the Father was acting as well. I don't believe that is correct. I believe that Jesus was teaching here that some deeds, such as healing, are so certainly the will of the Father that we can also minister healing whenever we choose and know for certain that it is something the Father and Jesus approve of our doing. The "unless" that is bolded in the above scripture tells me that Jesus could initiate healing on His own because it was something that He has seen the Father do over and over again. I don't hesitate when someone asks me to pray for their healing. I don't have to take time to ask the Father if this is something He wants me to do. I know it is His will, and I proceed with that knowledge.

Not only did Jesus heal the sick, He taught His disciples how to heal; and He expected them to be able to minister to people effectively. His instructions are recorded in Luke 9 and 10 as well as Matthew 10. He didn't make it complicated. He just told His disciples to do it, to *"heal the sick."* As Westerners, we have a tendency to need models instead of taking Jesus at His word and just doing it. When we lay our hands on the sick and minister healing, it is an exercise in faith; not faith in ourselves, but faith in the Lord to back us up in what He told us to do.

HEALING AND DELIVERANCE FUNDAMENTALS

When Jesus came down from the mountain after His transfiguration, He came across the father with the epileptic son. The disciples could not handle the situation; and Jesus was exasperated with them, not with the father. I sometimes wonder if He has the same feelings with the church today because there are so many sick and suffering in our midst and we seem impotent to change the situations.

Another reason we know that God wants to heal the sick is that we frequently see Him heal someone of a condition of which we were unaware; something that we didn't know about and didn't pray about. Here are a couple of examples:

> Several years ago, Scott and Kathy would drive to Kansas City from Chicago for weekend services at the fellowship of believers that at that time was named Kansas City Fellowship. My wife and I served on the pastoral staff of KCF and often ministered after services to those who requested it. Kathy had asked me for prayer and received a powerful touch from the Lord. She was so excited that the Lord had ministered to her that she wanted me to pray for her husband, Scott's, back. She hurried across the auditorium to bring, actually drag, Scott over for prayer. Scott didn't really know what was happening, and I was uncomfortable with the situation as I wasn't at all sure that he wanted me to pray for his back. So, there we were, two uncomfortable men and one excited lady. Scott agreed to receive prayer, so I quickly prayed for his back to be healed and left the scene. A couple of weeks later, Scott and Kathy returned to Kansas City and Scott informed us that yes, his back had been healed; but in addition to that healing, he was now able to raise his arm overhead. He discovered this when he returned to Chicago and was in a worship service and realized his arms were raised above his head in praise to the Lord! Scott had received surgery several years prior with the result that he no longer had full range of motion in his arm.

Another amazing healing story came about on our first trip to India. Doris and I are part of the International Association of Healing Rooms, and it was our privilege to travel to India to assist with starting healing rooms there. On our first visit, we ministered to Anthony, one of the team members in the healing rooms in Mumbai. Anthony was diabetic and had lost most of his vision; he was led about from place to place by the hand. We prayed for his vision, and it did improve; however, not as well as we all would have liked to see. However, Anthony received a major miracle in his foot. Years ago Anthony had worked as a painter; he had slipped off a ladder and run a piece of tile up into his foot. The foot became infected. To keep the infection from running up his leg, the lower part of Anthony's foot was surgically removed. We did not know that and we did not bring that situation before the Lord. The Lord in His goodness restored Anthony's foot to wholeness overnight. When Anthony awoke the next morning, he had a whole foot! It was a creative miracle. God put the rest of Anthony's foot back on. Why would God do this if He did not want to heal?

In Mark 16:18 Jesus said that healing the sick would be one of the signs that would accompany His followers. I know that some folks have trouble with this passage as it isn't included in some of the earliest manuscripts. To me that makes it all the more interesting. If the early church added it for some reason, it just makes it more evident that healing was a part of what the early church considered normal and essential. It is clear that the early church believed in divine healing and they practiced it. We can see this recorded in several passages in Acts and by reference to healing in some of the other New Testament letters. Not only did the early church practice healing, they taught it to others (see Acts 10:38). This is important because it clearly shows that they considered healing the sick to be a normal part of Christian life. It may surprise you to discover that the early church initially healed *all*, even as Jesus healed *all* who came to Him (see Acts 5:16). In a later chapter I will discuss some of the reasons everyone we minister to currently is not healed.

Additionally, my spirit bears witness to the goodness of healing and the degradation of sickness. Jesus told us that He would send us the Spirit of truth who would lead us into all the truth (John 16:13). My inner man bears witness with the Holy Spirit that healing is good. If I thought sickness was beneficial, I should desire it for myself and my family. I've never heard anyone ask God to make them sick! Just the contrary, I cry out in opposition to sickness when it strikes. I remember when I heard that Sharon, one of our dear friends, had been diagnosed with an aggressive form of leukemia. I immediately cried out, "No!" I knew, just knew, that this wasn't our Father's best for Sharon. We'll say more about Sharon in a later chapter, as her healing is a wonderful example of the goodness of God.

And finally, God made my body with "built-in" healing capabilities. He designed us so we would heal normally from most common illnesses and injuries. If I bruise my knee or cut my finger, I don't necessarily need to go to a physician or emergency room in the hospital. I know from experience that minor injuries or sicknesses will be healed normally with time. My body has an immune system to fight harmful viruses and bacteria which can cause sickness. It also has a wonderful ability to heal itself from cuts and bruises. If God wasn't in the healing business, He wouldn't have made our bodies with the recuperative powers they have.

I do believe that it is possible for God to use sickness to further His purpose or work in the life of the believer. I don't agree with the theology that says, "God can't make you sick; He isn't sick." The Bible tells me that all things are possible with God (Matthew 19:26), and that includes the ability to use sickness for good. There are a few recorded biblical instances where God caused physical infirmity to come onto an individual, such as Miriam's leprosy and Paul's blindness (see Numbers 12 and Acts 9). In these cases, both Miriam and Paul were physically obstructing God's will, and both of these situations were temporary as the individual was *physically* removed from hindering God's purpose. This seems to be the pattern in the few recorded instances where God initiates the infirmity, although it isn't always temporary, as Ananias and Sapphira and the Egyptians found out (Acts 5:1-11; Exodus 12:29-30).

Even though it is God's intention for us to be healed, that doesn't mean that the healing always occurs when we minister. Both the minister and the person seeking healing need to present themselves in a relaxed manner without any pressure to try and make something happen. If you are sick or hurting, we want to pray for you with the expectation that something good will happen. If it doesn't happen now, maybe it will in an hour, or tomorrow, or next week. You might be one prayer or one day away from your healing. Many healings are not instantaneous (see Mark 16:18); that can be seen in the natural and it is also true for supernatural healing. When improvement is experienced at the time of the healing prayer, often the complete healing occurs within a short time later. We know what will happen if we don't ask God to heal; so let's contend for what He desires for us. We will discuss this in more detail later.

In any event, I still believe that it is God's *normal* will to be for our healing and against our sickness or infirmity. There are only a few biblical instances where God initiates the sickness, and the healings attributed to His goodness and initiative were too numerous to all be recorded. John's last verse (21:25) in his Gospel tells us:

And there are also many other things which Jesus did, which if they were written in detail, I suppose that even the world itself would not contain the books which were written.

Doris and I have found this to be the case, even for us. From time to time we also endeavor to record the healings we see, but most of the time we just remember the ones that have some unusual element in them. A case in point is a healing of a young man's back in a cold Minneapolis parking lot. As several people gathered to pray for his back, we could hear the bones crackling as they moved into a different position. Also, right over his right shoulder blade, exactly where he had experienced an injury, a "hot spot" developed that could be felt through his leather jacket. People took turns laying their hands on the warm spot on his jacket, which was in sharp contrast to the remainder of his jacket that was exposed to the cold Minnesota night air. Isn't God interesting?

Healing of Animals

We don't note any biblical stories about God healing animals; but His nature is healing, so why would He not? On several occasions we have found that God responds to our requests for healing for animals. I will relate a couple of those incidents here.

Our son Tim found a stray cat and wanted to keep it for a pet. We were reluctant to accommodate this request, but allowed him to keep the cat as long as it stayed outside. We already had an indoor cat—my daughter's pet, named Puff. Tim named the cat Brutus; and he was a friendly, personable animal. He used to climb to the top of a small tree we had in our front yard where his weight would cause the top of the tree to swing back and forth; he looked so silly.

We lived in South Dakota, and both cold and hot temperatures can prevail in that state at times. Sometimes summer temperatures could reach more than 100 degrees Fahrenheit, and in the winter they could drop to minus 20 degrees Fahrenheit or less. Brutus had only been around a few days when the weather turned bitterly cold, and it appeared that he had frozen his tail. It just dragged on the ground behind him. Tim, a teenager, could pinch the tail as hard as he could and Brutus did not show that he felt any pain. In that part of South Dakota, you could sometimes see cattle with only part of a tail or perhaps missing part of an ear. It had been frozen and then dropped off. Doris prayed, "*O God, You know how I feel about this cat, but I don't think I could handle it if his tail falls off.*" She prayed for his tail, and God healed it.

God can heal larger animals too. Below is Deb's story of how God healed her horse—a very expensive, special animal to be used as a jumper. When Deb first shared about her injured horse, she was concerned that it may have to be put down as the damage was possibly severe enough to make her unsafe and not useable as a jumper. Here is the story as written by Deb:

> I had just gotten a new horse that had been raised in Canada and had no experience of a large urban boarding facility. She became very frightened of a twenty-foot rollup door as I was moving her from the arena back into a stall. The noise and movement scared her so bad that she bolted free from me; and when she couldn't go back into the arena, she ran between the steel beams of the building and the wall. We had to take the wall apart to get her out. She had ripped her hide open on both shoulders and walked three-legged, in a lot of pain. The vet was already on an emergency call and said it would be three hours before he could get there. He directed us to just make her comfortable and quiet with little

movement in a stall until he could determine the extent of the damage to her shoulders.

Once she was settled, I went to a healing prayer service that was scheduled at my church, as I wanted specific prayers for a friend with cancer. Lee Harms greeted me and saw how distraught I was, so I recounted the accident my new horse had just had and that I was waiting to know the full extent of her injuries. Lee prayed for her.

Later in the evening when the Vet finally got there, her open wounds seemed to have shrunk, and to this day a one-inch circle of white hair is the only reminder of any injury; but more importantly, she walked out and x-rayed sound—no damage to her shoulder, even though she had originally been so sore we suspected she had either dislocated or chipped her shoulder against the steel beam of the barn.

Thanks be to God for those healing prayers for my horse!

How Does God Heal?

The tongue in cheek answer to the above question, of course, is, "Any way He wants to." Jesus demonstrated healing in a variety of ways, but frequently He just laid His hand on the individual He was ministering to (Luke 4:40). This seems to be the most natural way to minister healing for me; simply the "laying on of hands," i.e., touching the person as we seek for the healing to come. We all need to use discretion, of course, in where we lay our hands, especially when we are ministering to someone of the opposite sex. If we pray for someone who has a physical ailment in a sensitive location, I can lay my hand on their shoulder or touch their forehead as we pray. God can still do the healing. It does seem to help raise the faith level if we can lay our hands near the affected part of the body, so frequently we will ask the individual requesting prayer to lay *their* hand on the particular area involved and we then lay our hand on top of theirs.

There are many healing stories that we could tell from laying our hands on someone with a particular sickness, but one of my favorites occurred in the base hospital at Ellsworth Air Force Base near Rapid City, South Dakota. Doris and I had received a telephone call asking us to pray for a lady who was hospitalized and seriously ill. She and her husband were from out of town, but she was entitled to military benefits as he was retired military. When we visited her, we could see she was in very rough shape. I don't remember all the problems she was having, but I remember that kidney failure was one of them. She knew the Lord, and I remember that Doris asked her if she even wanted us to pray for healing or if she just wanted to go home and be with the Lord. She wanted us to ask for healing, so we ministered to her and then left.

The following week we were back at that same hospital to pray for a different lady, and we decided to stop and visit the woman we had prayed for previously, but she wasn't there. We asked the nurse regarding her situation, and the nurse informed us that she had "been discharged." Our level of faith for her healing was not very high, so Doris and I didn't ask for any further details. We thought she may have died, and we left the hospital without knowing whether the woman had been discharged vertically or horizontally! Sometime later we received a post card from the lady and her husband. God had touched her body, and they were on their way back to their home in California. What makes this story so interesting to me is that when we prayed, the Lord opened a deaf ear that she had been unable to hear out of for thirty-two years. We didn't pray for this ear to be opened; we didn't even know she had a bad ear, as we were asking for other life threatening situations to be rectified. I think of this story, and others like it, when I fall into the trap of thinking my words have to be so exact to enable a healing to happen. God just did it! All we did was lay our hands on her and pray; He is so good!

Another common way that Jesus healed was through the use of the word of knowledge. This is an effective way for the Holy Spirit to initiate a healing, and we have been blessed to receive many of these words as we have been in a position to minister the healing. One week at our Saturday evening worship service, I received a word for healing of a thirty-four-year-old woman with a heart murmur. The word of knowledge will be discussed in more detail in a later chapter, but having some specifics about the person helps identify who it is that the Lord wants to touch. Even though there were several hundred people at the service, there was only one thirty-four-year-old woman with a heart murmur.

Jesus sometimes used His spit as a healing vehicle (Mark 7:33); but this would offend most people today, so we don't recommend it unless you specifically believe that God is directing you to minister in this fashion. Jesus always wants us to treat those we minister to with kindness and respect. Another way that healing is administered is by anointing the sick person with oil. We don't have any indication that Jesus ever did this, but the disciples used oil (Mark 6:13) and it is mentioned by James as a method used by the elders of the early church (James 5:14). Oil is a type or symbol of the Holy Spirit; and it is not necessary to use it, as Christians have the in-dwelling Holy Spirit present with them as they minister. Conversely, there isn't any reason not to use oil; and we have found it to be a help on occasion, especially when ministering to someone who has been involved in some sort of occult practice. I have found that demons rooted in the occult hate the use of oil. If they hate it; I like it.

Oil was used by the pastor during the first major healing that Doris and I observed. A friend of ours, who I will call Mary, had injured her back by falling on her deck. She was emotionally upset anyway, as her husband had just left her and their two small children and it looked as if they were headed for divorce. The spinal column had shifted when she fell, causing pressure on the sciatic nerve resulting in numbness in her right leg, lack of motor skills, and much pain. Mary's doctor diagnosed a ruptured disc and recommended immediate surgery.

Mary wasn't willing to have surgery in a hurry and wanted to submit herself to the Lord for healing first. She called several of us to come pray for her. She was in such pain that she lay on the bed while she was anointed with oil and prayed over. I can still recall kneeling by the side of the bed with my hands on the covers over Mary's bad leg (something that I no longer would deem appropriate). As we all prayed, Mary's body started moving vertically, up and down, as the power of the Holy Spirit came upon her. I remember feeling the movement and opening my eyes to see what was happening. Mary was as astonished as I was. Try laying down somewhere and moving your body up and down. You can't do it on your own power. Mary's healing was immediate. The pain left, she got up, her leg was functional; and within minutes we left her and the children alone, all of us praising the Lord for His goodness in healing Mary.

Within a few hours, Mary was once again down in bed, in pain, and the disc once again seemed to have returned to its damaged position. We went back to pray for Mary, and the Lord touched her again. As before, she could get up at once and resume her normal duties. This scenario was repeated once more before we decided that after prayer Mary should simply rest for a couple of days before trying to put her back to the test of normal living. After all, the doctor had told Mary that she would have to stay in bed for a long period after the surgery so resting the back for a couple of days after prayer seemed reasonable. This worked, and Mary never did have to have surgery. She jogs, skis, and leads a normal and active life. We learned something important from this healing—the healing may be a process even when God does it and it seems as if it were an immediate miracle.

Another way that the Lord heals is through the use of prayer cloths (see Acts 19:11-12). Charles and Frances Hunter tell the very miraculous story of an English baby who was healed when a cloth they had prayed over was laid on him. They had gathered their office staff in Houston to pray over the cloth and then had mailed it to England. They like to think of all the people that had handled the envelope before it got to its destination and how that process didn't hinder God in any way. We have some wonderful results from prayer cloths also. Kevin, who ministers with our healing teams, had a friend who had suffered from the effects of a spider bite for five years. The bite affected an area the size of a teacup saucer and an area the size of a silver dollar bled continuously. After one and one-half days of laying the cloth on the afflicted area, there was much improvement. It didn't smell anymore, and both the infected area and the weeping decreased substantially. The infected area continued to heal.

Even though we have used "prayer" as a means of describing how we minister to the sick, often times it isn't really prayer *per se*. Jesus didn't tell us to "pray for the sick," He just told us to do it. I will share more about this later. Mark 11:23-24 speaks of a kind of faith that can move mountains. I understand this to be an unusual confidence that God will act in a certain situation. This confidence is sometimes dropped into a believer's heart, as a gift from the Holy Spirit, to accomplish something in particular. The something that is accomplished can be a healing, and you will often hear us speak directly to body parts and command them to be whole, etc. We've experienced some wonderful healings when new parts, such as hearts, have been commanded to come into place. Obviously, I don't know if a new heart actually is installed by the Lord or if He repairs the old one. I do know that several people with heart problems no longer experience difficulties.

One elderly lady whose heart responded to ministry was Mrs. Crandle who came to our Lutheran prayer group for prayer one evening. She hadn't been able to get out much, was unable to do her own housework, and in general was leading a very restricted life. During the worship time, before we ministered to her, she sat away from the rest of the group near the window as she felt very short of breath and was experiencing respiratory difficulties. We prayed for her soon after we were through worship, and she left for home without staying for the rest of the evening.

We didn't hear any more from Mrs. Crandle for several weeks; then one night she again showed up at our Monday night prayer meeting. She was excited; she was so much better. She had traveled to the East Coast to see her children and grandchildren; then she had gone to the West Coast to do the same. She was doing her own housework and leading a much more active life. She gave the Lord the praise, and so did we!

We also know that Jesus sometimes addressed a spirit prior to administering His healing touch (see Luke 13:11-13). In fact, while both the Gospels Matthew and Luke mention that Jesus gave the disciples authority to cast out demons and to heal diseases (see Luke 9:1 and Matthew 10:1), in Mark's Gospel only the authority over demons is mentioned as they departed on their journey to preach the gospel and heal the sick. Sometimes the importance of dealing with demons as we minister to the sick is overlooked. Doris and I seldom saw asthma healed when we first began ministering to those suffering from this ailment. We learned that a respiratory spirit or spirit of asthma often either causes the disease or hinders the healing. Now we address the spirit behind this illness first, and then speak healing into the respiratory system. We estimate that currently approximately 80 percent of the asthmatics receiving ministry are healed using this approach. Authority over demons will be more fully addressed in Part II of this work.

We have several examples of people healed using the approach described in the preceding paragraph. Perhaps one of the most dramatic healings was the healing of Debra Winter's sister, Bobi. Doris and I had been invited to minister at a Women's Aglow meeting in Manhattan, Kansas. As we prepared for the meeting, I felt the Holy Spirit was indicating that someone would need to be set free from a spirit in order to obtain their healing (see Luke 13:11-13) and that the disease was likely related to the respiratory system. Prior to the meeting, Doris was talking with Debra, who shared about all the respiratory problems within her family. Debra felt the Lord had healed her asthma, a child within the family had been lost to respiratory failure, and her sister, Bobi, was currently in ICU at a Phoenix area hospital and was not expected to recover. Bobi had contacted pneumonia, had deteriorated with a variety of respiratory complications, and had been in ICU for six weeks. During the meeting I called Debra forward for ministry, broke the generational curse of respiratory infirmity, and prayed for healing for both Debra and Bobi. The spirit manifested in a physical way on Debra as it left, and she immediately felt she could breathe easier. The amazing thing, however, is that by the next day her sister, still in ICU in Arizona, sat up in her bed and indicated she was thirsty and hungry. At this time Bobi was on a ventilator, had a tracheotomy and a stoma, and was receiving oxygen. The vent was removed; Bobi could breathe on her own and was on the way to a rapid recovery. She remained in the hospital as she regained her strength. She was later released without the need for any oxygen supplementation or rehabilitation. In Debra's words: "God has healed my sister COMPLETELY! Hallelujah! HE is faithful and true! Marvelous is His name in all the earth, and above the earth! HE is the God who still performs miracles today."

Let's finish this chapter with another healing testimony. The testimony below is as received from Susan:

> Friday January 15, 1993, is one of the days that changed my life. I was working as a florist at the time. A co-worker and I were taking down Christmas decorations in the greenhouse when he decided to swing on a twelve-foot section of pipe that was hanging over my head. The hooks holding the pipe in place gave way and the pipe and the weight of my co-worker came crashing down on my right shoulder.
>
> This accident left me in severe pain for the next eighteen years, and the damage to my shoulder was so severe I had to quit my job

and give up many of the things I enjoyed doing because of the pain. The accident could not have happened at a worse time. I had just been asked to run a floral shop for a friend of mine who wanted to open a new business in the small town where I was living. I wasn't sure if I should go into business with him or go back to school and finish my undergraduate degree. I didn't have a really strong relationship with God at the time, but had decided to fast and pray about my future on the day of the accident. Over the years I often forgot to consider that I was asking God to show me which direction I should take in my future, and instead I began to blame God for destroying my shoulder.

Over the next eighteen years I had many people pray for me, anoint me, and pronounce healing over my shoulder, but to no avail. The pain remained and several areas of scar tissue built up along my shoulder blade making it impossible some days to stand upright. In 2010 my relationship with God and Jesus was changed when I came on staff at T!LC. One of the most significant changes in my relationship with Christ grew out of my participation in Cleansing Stream and the silent retreat. During those events I learned how to trust more fully in God again, and over the next year physical healing began to happen in my body as I surrendered more and more of myself to God.

On Friday, February 25, 2011, while attending a discussion group at the home of Doris and Lee Harms, I came forward for healing prayers. I have to admit I was a bit skeptical. I had gone forward for healing prayers for my back many times over the years and I wasn't sure this time would be any different. I stood before Lee and Doris and they had such a calming effect on me. They were not pretentious at all. When they prayed for me, they barely touched my body; but yet it was moving and I felt the distinct presence of the Holy Spirit come upon me. I had never felt this before when others had prayed for my back. During the prayer time I did not feel any immediate relief from the pain; however, Lee anointed me with oil and prayed against the spirit of pain which could have taken up residency around me because I had suffered with chronic pain for so many years.

That next day I awoke and the headache I had been suffering from for several weeks seemed to have disappeared, and I was excited for the relief. I went about my prayer time at IHOP as scheduled, did homework on my computer all the way home from Kansas City, and attended our regular CMA functions that night. When I got home around 7:00 that evening, I immediately went into my office and began typing/working on my paper that was due the following Monday. Around 2:00 a.m. Sunday morning, I stopped the work that I had been doing. I realized I had been typing for over seven hours straight without a break and for the first time ever I didn't have any pain in my back. I sat in my chair staring at the keyboard wondering what was going on. Normally if I was working that long at the computer I would have had a heating pad and Biofreeze on my back and I would have consumed about 2,000 milligrams of Ibuprofen; but I hadn't done anything and there was no pain. Since I was at a natural stopping point in my paper and I had work later that morning at church, I went to bed and slept well (which was also not normal for me). When I awoke later that morning, I noticed the pain was still gone.

I told Rich I thought God had healed my back, but I wasn't sure what was going on. I wasn't sure if I should tell anyone, not knowing if it was real or not. I didn't want to jinx anything that might have happened, but later that morning I found myself telling Pastor Bruce about the healing. He just looked at me with a strange look on his face. I couldn't tell what was going on with him, and then he asked me if I understood how significant this healing was. I wasn't sure what he was talking about until he told me, "You mean you are telling me that you have been in pain every day for more than eighteen years and now today after the Harms prayed over you, you have no pain. Is that what you are saying?" I stood there a minute and then the enormity of the healing hit me.

A couple of days later I had a chance to get a massage on my back. Normally this isn't a really fun thing for me since I had many pockets of scar tissue throughout my shoulder area and it was always very painful for the therapist to massage those areas. As I lay on the table that morning, I waited for the pain to come. The therapist placed her thumbs on each side of my spine and began to massage the full length of my spinal column and then out toward my right shoulder. There was no pain!!! There was no scar tissue!!! It was completely healed. I couldn't wait to tell people what had happened. God had reached down from heaven that day in Kansas City and had completely, totally, healed my back. For many weeks afterwards I waited for the pain to come back, but eventually I realized God had done a mighty work in me that day. I was HEALED by the hand of the Savior Jesus Christ, by the power of the Holy Spirit who came upon me and restored the broken tissues and nerves in my back!!!! Praise the Lord, hallelujah; the Lord is good.

CHAPTER 2

The Healing Word and the Authority to Heal the Sick

As was learned in chapter 1, God is for healing. He has commissioned the church and given her the authority to carry out His will here on earth. Just as Jesus gave the disciples power and authority to heal the sick and cast out demons, the same power and authority are available to believers everywhere today.

About 700 years before Jesus was born, the prophet Isaiah predicted a Messiah would come to Israel and carry our sickness and pain (Isaiah 53:4, literal translation, margin NASB). He would be pierced for our transgressions (sin), crushed for our iniquities (our desire to sin), chastened for our well-being (opposite of oppression), and scourged for our healing. Thus, the Messiah, Christ, would save us from our sin, our sicknesses, and demonic oppression. God made total provision through the atonement of Christ. Through the suffering and crucifixion of Jesus, we can receive forgiveness for our transgressions, healing for our diseases, and deliverance from demonic oppression. By and large, the Western church has lost sight of much of what Jesus obtained for us on the cross. Matthew, in his Gospel, affirms the reality of being saved from sin, sickness, and demonic oppression. He specifically writes that Jesus cast out the spirits and healed all who were ill in order to fulfill what Isaiah spoke seven centuries before (see Matthew 8:15-16).

Also recorded in the eighth chapter of Matthew are two important stories of healing. In the first, a leper asks Jesus if He is willing to heal him. The leper had probably watched Jesus heal others but knew that he was an outcast and wondered, "Would you heal even me?" Jesus leaves no doubt regarding this issue, He immediately responds: "*I am willing; be cleansed.*" (Matthew 8:3). This is the only place is scripture where Jesus is asked if He is willing to heal and His immediate response is, "Yes, I will!" The second healing recorded here is in response to a centurion's request for healing of his paralyzed servant boy. Jesus is willing to travel to the boy and heal him; He knows that He can do this. The servant boy is healed without Jesus making the trip, but note two important facts from these two stories:

1. Jesus is willing to heal (Matthew 8:3), and
2. Jesus is able to heal (v. 7).

The writer of Hebrews affirms the unchanging nature of God by stating that "*Jesus Christ is the same yesterday and today and forever*" (Hebrews 13:8). God is perfect; and if someone is perfect, they cannot change from their perfection and still remain perfect. We can be assured that it is Jesus' will today to heal. He cannot change His mind now; His atoning work is already done. If you purchased an automobile from a dealer and drove that car for two years, you would not expect to be able to return it to the dealer and receive your money back. You already had made the decision to purchase and use that particular auto; you could not change your mind later. God has already made the decision that the atoning work of His Son on the cross is sufficient to rectify all that the enemy has put on mankind regarding sin, sickness, and demonic oppression.

Let's take a moment to look at something else in these verses from Matthew that's very interesting. In Matthew 8:16 he records that *all* were healed. Several other verses in the New Testament likewise indicate that Jesus healed all who came to Him. Consider a crowd for a moment. Some came seeking healing from this One who had healed others. Others were hopeful that they could be healed; others were doubtful; and still others were likely very skeptical and even critical. Some probably came just to see what was happening where the crowd was forming without any thought of being healed at all. Yet, Jesus healed them *all*. Clearly the responsibility for being healed did not rest on those who came; they simply needed to present themselves for His touch.

Our Authority to Heal

I've believed that Christians had the authority from God to heal the sick for many years, but I didn't really understand it. One day in India as I was preparing to minister this particular aspect of the work, I finally understood the basis for having the authority to heal. Knowing how we receive this authority will increase your confidence as you minister to the sick.

In the first chapter of Genesis, God blessed man (male and female, v. 27) and told them: "*Be fruitful and multiply, and fill the earth, and subdue it; and rule over the fish of the sea and over the birds of the sky and over every living thing that moves on the earth*" (v. 28). Just to emphasize, God told them to (1) be fruitful, (2) multiply, (3) rule, and (4) subdue. Most of us are familiar with how the original creation deteriorated to a point that God regretted He had made man on earth (6:6). Man's wickedness resulted in judgment by the flood with only Noah, his three sons, their wives, and Noah's wife saved from the waters that covered the earth. After Noah exited the ark and gave a burnt offering on the altar he constructed, the Lord once again issued His blessing and commandment, "*Be fruitful and multiply, and fill the earth*" (9:1, 7). When God's command to Noah is compared to the previous command to Adam, this question arises: what happened to rule and subdue?

Adam's authority to rule and subdue on the earth (not in heaven) was stolen from him by Satan when he agreed with Satan and rebelled against God's authority to restrict him from eating of the tree of the knowledge of good and evil. Thus lawlessness entered into man's relationship with God as he denied the Almighty's right to govern his affairs. Note that Satan stole the right to rule and subdue, he did not steal ownership. The earth and all it contains still belongs to its Maker (Psalm 24:1; Exodus 9:29). An analogy to this situation would be if a thief stole my automobile. While it was in his possession, he would rule it; he could drive it anywhere he chose and even wreck it if he was so inclined. However, the minute the thief was apprehended by the authorities, the auto would be returned to me as I had retained ownership even during the time I was no longer in control of it.

The New Testament confirms Satan as ruler of the earth. When Jesus was tempted by Satan after He returned from the wilderness, Satan declared that all the kingdoms of the world had been handed over to him and if Jesus would only worship him, he would return them to Jesus. Jesus did not deny Satan's claim of ownership. In fact, in both John 12:31 and 14:30, Jesus acknowledges this right to rule and identifies Satan as "the ruler of this world."

Jesus also had the right to rule and subdue the earth along with Satan, as He received His authority to do so directly from the Father as the second sinless man; Adam before the fall being the first. Paul gives us this information in 1 Corinthians 15:45-47. So, when Jesus appeared on the scene, earth suddenly had two rulers. One ruler had destruction in mind and the other desired to see the kingdom of heaven established on earth. One ruled for evil and the other for good. Earth was in conflict, but Jesus won every conflict. The devil stirred up the water with a storm, and Jesus calmed it. The devil put sickness and disease on people, and Jesus healed all who came to Him for healing. Acts 10:38 tells us the Jesus *"went about doing good and healing all who were oppressed by the devil."*

When Jesus went to the cross, He atoned for Adam's sin just as He atoned for yours and mine. He bought back Adam's original authority to rule and subdue; and now He has His authority, given by the Father, in addition to Adam's original authority which was stolen by the devil. This atoning act gave Jesus the right, after His resurrection, to declare, *"All authority has been given to Me in heaven and earth"* (Matthew 28:18). His next word is directed to us, He says, *"Go"* (v. 19). We understand that He is sending us under His authority and in His name. We are to be His ambassadors (2 Corinthians 5:20). An ambassador serves at the pleasure of his government and must abide by his government's policies and directives; he can't make new policies on his own. Yet, an ambassador knows if he acts prudently and under his government's authority that the full support and strength of his government will stand behind him. That's the way it is, or should be, with Christians. As we become ambassadors for Christ and operate under His authority and direction from His Spirit, we can be confident that the full strength of heaven is behind us. If we need help, we can ask and receive it.

Several verses in the New Testament still refer to Satan's influence and power in the world. For instance, 2 Corinthians 4:4 calls Satan the *"god of this world,"* and 1 John 5:19 states, *"The whole world lies in the power of the evil one."* We must remember that we are *in* the world, but not *of* the world (John 15:19). When we are born of God, we overcome the world (1 John 5:4). And, remember that *"greater is He who is in you than he who is in the world"* (1 John 4:4).

God Wants to Make Believers out of Believers

Centuries of doubt and unbelief have hindered today's church in stepping into the things that God has for us. In our heads we believe that Jesus commanded us to spread the gospel, heal the sick, free the demonized, and even raise the dead. Yet within our hearts, we doubt our ability to fulfill these commands. We may believe that someone, somewhere, is equipped or anointed to see these deeds come to reality; but we are unsure that God can or will use us to accomplish such marvelous events.

Actually, we can't do these things; they are supernatural occurrences and can only happen because we are in direct relationship with a supernatural God. Primarily because we have not seen the results we desire when we pray, Satan has been able to sow these seeds of doubt and unbelief throughout the church. We need to say with Saint Paul, *"Not that we are adequate in ourselves to consider anything as coming from ourselves, but our adequacy is from God"* (2 Corinthians 3:5). Somehow we have come to believe that it is normal for Satan to be able to make us sick but it is not normal for God to be able to make us well. Many times we curse ourselves by speaking against what is written in God's Word, and we get what we say. An anointed healing evangelist, the late Frances Hunter, told how she used to catch the flu every season. She knew she was susceptible to it and would say, "Well, flu season is coming, so I'm going to catch the flu pretty soon." And she would. After she understood her authority as a child of God, she changed her attitude and what she spoke. She said she never had the flu again and lived into her nineties. I'm as guilty as anyone in not paying attention to what I'm saying. Joyce Meyer, in her book *Battlefield of the Mind*, stresses that we need to think about what we are thinking about. This makes good common sense because:

What I think determines what I say,

What I say determines what I believe, and

What I believe determine what I am and what I will do.

Healing is the work of the body of Christ. Jesus commanded us, among other things, to heal the sick (Matthew 10:8). He expects us to activate healing based on His promises and His command. I used to teach engineering students at a major university. As part of the learning experience, we often had laboratory experiments designed to reinforce the concepts being taught in the classroom. It was not unusual for a team of students to seek my assistance in interpreting their laboratory results because the outcome was different from expected based on the theory given to them in class. Never once in my eighteen years as a college professor did I tell them I would write the author of the textbook to inform him that his theory was incorrect based on my student's laboratory results. No, I was able to point out possible changes in procedure that would help them obtain better results. They would return to the laboratory, rerun the experiment, and gain better understanding of both the theory and proper laboratory procedures. Too often within the church we abandon ministering to the sick because of our lack of success. We need to reread the textbook (the Bible), consult the author (the Holy Spirit), and try it again. The more we do, the more healings we will witness. When my wife and I first began ministering to the sick some thirty-five years ago, we saw less than 10 percent of the sick healed through prayer. It is impossible to specify an accurate percentage, but it appears that we now see at least 50 percent of those receiving ministry either healed or improved.

We have been taught doubt and unbelief, and the antidote to both doubt and unbelief is faith. Faith is an issue; we tend to believe what we see in the natural more than what God says in His book. In *The Heavens Opened*, Anna Rountree writes of her heavenly experiences where she was exposed to a class of healing angels being readied for release on the earth. As Anna addressed the trainees, she indicated that most believers have a difficult time believing in divine healing. The angels were stunned into silence before they responded with such statements as, "It is a covenant promise. By His stripes He has knit you back or mended or joined you again to Him who is divine health. It is sure."[1]

Faith

We all need more faith. Jesus commended both the centurion in Matthew 8 and the woman healed of the hemorrhage in Matthew 9 for their faith. Note that their faith was in the Son of God not within themselves. We need to develop this attitude as well.

There are two kinds of faith: (1) saving faith, and (2) the gift of faith. Let's explore these two kinds of faith in more detail. Every believer has a measure of faith (Romans 12:3). We can't even become a believer without some faith in Jesus by the Holy Spirit. This faith can grow (2 Thessalonians 1:3), and it is our responsibility to nurture it. The second kind of faith, the gift of faith, is just that—a gift. It is given by the Holy Spirit (1 Corinthians 12:9) to accomplish God's purpose at a specific time and place. It's the kind of faith that moves mountains (Mark 11:23-24); and it cannot be activated as we desire, only as God desires. It's actually a time when someone is allowed to use some of God's faith. When you experience the gift of faith, you know that whatever you are praying about will come to pass.

I've only experienced the gift of faith a few times. The most vivid memory I have of an incident where a gift of faith was activated occurred when I was fishing with my wife. Doris and I like to relax by fishing, and many years ago we had a family vacation planned with our two children and Doris' mother. We rented a small cabin and a small aluminum fishing boat for a week on Roy Lake, a glacial lake in northeast South Dakota. As we checked into the resort and picked up the boat, we noticed how windy it was and the high waves that the wind was generating on the lake. The resort owner said that it had been that way for some time now and fishing on the lake with a small boat, such as we had, was just not feasible unless the wind went down. We did try to get out onto the lake later that afternoon; but, as the owner had said, it was just too windy. We thought that perhaps the wind would not be blowing early in the morning, so the next day we got up

---

1   Anna Rountree, *The Heavens Opened* (St. Mary's, FL: Creation House, 1999), 29.

at about 4 a.m. to go fishing. As we tried to enter the main lake from the small sheltered cove where our boat and cabin were located, it just didn't work. I was afraid we would capsize the boat. We fished in the small cove for awhile, but it was futile. The cove was only about three to four feet deep and fishing was not productive. Suddenly, something (a gift of faith) rose up in Doris. She said, "Point me toward the lake." She was sitting in the bow of the small boat, and I was running the motor at the rear. I cautiously started toward the main lake; and as I did, I heard her saying, "Wind be still." She was a little tentative about it at first, but soon became more confident and spoke the words with authority. To my surprise the lake started to become calmer; and as we went further out into the lake, it became calmer still. We fished on calm waters that morning and continued to do so the entire week we were at the resort. On the final day, we fished on calm waters in the morning and returned to the cabin about midmorning to pack up our things in preparation for departure by noon. In order to return the boat to the resort, I had to once again go from the cove onto the main lake. As I did so, I could tell that the wind was picking up again and it almost was at the point that I could not safely navigate back to the resort dock. God was faithful as He honored the faith that Doris used while we had our vacation week; but those coming after us had to once again combat windy waves.

We can't call a gift of faith into action; that's the Holy Spirit's job. However, we can ask Him for more frequent use of this gift. And we can nurture the faith each believer is given when he makes his commitment to Jesus and asks Him to be Lord of his life. We can cultivate the soil of our heart, let the seed of the word go deep within, and spend time with the Lord and His people. We can use the tools of prayer, prayer in the Spirit, fasting, worship, and study of the Word to help our faith grow. One major way our faith grows is the sharing of testimonies of what God has done. The Christian church is weak in this area. For some reason we don't share the activity of God in our lives with others around us. I was at a meeting once when an acquaintance shared a testimony with me regarding his daughter being healed. I didn't remember the incident, but he said we had come to the hospital to pray for his newborn daughter who was suffering from serious heart defects. They weren't sure that she was going to survive. He said that she had been healed after our visit. I rejoiced with him, and then asked how old his daughter was now. "She's ten," he replied. I was astounded. Here was a major healing for his daughter that he had neglected to share with us for ten years!

Testimonies are very important in building up our faith. In 1 John 5:4 we learn that the victory that overcomes the world is our faith. In Romans 10:17 Paul says that faith comes by hearing the word "concerning" Christ (NASB margin). And finally in Revelation 12:11, we find the importance of testimony as we are overcomers by the blood of the Lamb and the word of our testimony. It becomes a cycle of building our faith regarding healing when we share testimonies about healing:

Overcomer shares testimony → Others hear testimony →
Builds faith up in all → Generates new testimonies to share

We don't have to have a history of healings behind us to step out in faith. Once I was helping teach a healing school and we saw a marvelous miracle from the hands of someone who was just exploring the possibility that God still healed. I was coaching one of the student attendees as she prayed for a man from Canada with a severe eye disability. Forceps had been used during his birth, and they had slipped and gone into his eye. His eye was badly damaged and pushed back into his head. As he grew he had multiple surgeries to move the eye forward and repair it as much as possible. With a contact lens he was able to discern shadows but was unable to see detail or to read, etc. After the student briefly prayed for healing for his eye, we asked him if he could see any difference. He replied, "No, everything is still blurry." Then he said, "Wait a moment," and he removed his contact lens. He was able to distinguish the words on some banners hung high in the church. This was an improvement, and by the next morning he was able to read his Bible without any visual assistance.

The church must begin to contend for healing; if we Christians don't, who will? We must learn to view healing with the same attitude we do for those answering the altar call for salvation. If someone comes forward and makes the decision to declare Jesus as his Lord, we say that he is saved; he has entered into the family of God. We don't wait to see if he has his act together to declare that he has become a believer. We understand that there are issues yet to be worked out in his life. Jesus cleans His fish after

He catches them. Yet, when someone comes forward for healing prayer, we pray and then wait to see if the healing is manifested in their body. Manifestations are nice, but they don't heal. The Word of God heals; the living Word, Jesus Christ. Let's trust Him to do what He said He can and will do. I'm preaching to myself here; I'm as guilty as anyone about wanting to see the manifestation of healing. But we are learning and trusting more. Most of the time when we minister to someone with pain, we expect the pain to leave. They should be able to move their arm or leg or whatever was paining them before ministry, and the pain should be gone because Jesus has healed them.

Romans 1:16 states that the gospel *"is the power of God for salvation to everyone who believes."* Remember that salvation as indicated in the Scriptures is a total salvation; we are saved from our sin, our sicknesses, and demonic oppression. The Greek word for this kind of salvation is *sozo*. It is translated into English depending upon the context in which it is used. For example, in Acts 2:21 we can be sure we are "saved" from our sins and transgressions by calling upon the Lord. Then, in Acts 14:9 Paul saw that a man who was listening to him had faith to be made well. The margin of our Bible indicates that literally this man was "saved." And finally, an example of being saved from demonic oppression is found in Luke 8:36 where the demonically oppressed man was made well. Again, the margin in our Bible indicates this man was actually "saved." All three of these examples have their origin in the root word *sozo*.

Why is the Bible more clear regarding salvation from sin than salvation from sickness and demonic oppression? I believe it is because it is the most important. Jesus seems to emphasize this in Mark 1:38 when He leaves Capernaum to preach elsewhere even though there are still needs to be met there. We cannot enter into eternity with Jesus without experiencing salvation, but we can enter into His presence after death if we haven't yet been physically healed or delivered from demonic oppression. That doesn't mean that we should forget about trying to heal the sick or minister deliverance to the oppressed. Jesus came to do all these things and commanded the church to continue His ministry until He returns. Many people will never accept Jesus so their sins are forgiven unless they first see the demonstration of His awesome power and majesty as He sets people free from sickness and oppression. Jesus told the church to heal because:

He seeks to destroy the works of the devil (1 John 3:8).

He has compassion of those who are downtrodden (Matthew 14:14).

It is His very nature to heal (Exodus 15:26).

It is a means of affirming the gospel to believers and unbelievers alike (John 20:30-31).

One of my favorite stories that came from the recent Lakeland, Florida, revival concerns a skeptical biker from the East Coast. He and his friends used to watch the revival for enjoyment, laughing and making sport of people falling under the power and testifying of being healed by the supernatural power of God. One day he and his friends decided that one of them should actually travel to Lakeland to check it out. They pooled their resources and this particular biker was selected to make the trip on their behalf and return with a report. He traveled down the East Coast on his Harley-Davidson motorcycle and came to the revival meeting. He ended up getting healed and saved and testifying to the goodness of God. God is good.

CHAPTER 3

The Anointing for Healing

Jesus openly declared His ministry when He visited the synagogue in His home town some eight to ten months after returning from His wilderness experience. He read the following scriptures from Isaiah, as is recorded in Luke 4:18-19:

> *The Spirit of the Lord is upon Me, because He anointed Me to preach the gospel to the poor. He has sent Me to proclaim release to the captives, and recovery of sight to the blind, to set free those who are oppressed, to proclaim the favorable year of the Lord.*

In the previous chapter we stressed the authority given to believers to heal the sick and demonized based on the Word of God. In this chapter we want to consider the anointing that empowers that Word. Some Christians primarily emphasize the authority from the Word while other Christians almost exclusively stress the anointing. Both are very important and both are necessary. They work together to accomplish the works of God.

What is this anointing that is so important to have? In 1 John 2:27 it is clear that this anointing, which comes directly from God, teaches you about all things. Earlier in his Gospel, the same author uses this same phraseology to refer to the Holy Spirit, *"But the helper, the Holy Spirit,...He will teach you all things"* (John 14:26). Thus, the anointing we seek is none other than the person of the Holy Spirit. The Holy Spirit comes *within* us forever

(John 14:16) when we become believers, but He also comes *upon* us when we are anointed and empowered for service. The anointing within me is for my good; the anointing upon me is for the good of others. The anointing is the presence and activity of the Holy Spirit. It is sometimes intangible, but also can sometimes be perceived—a presence is felt, someone feels heat or cold on their body, or they begin to shake or weep. These and other manifestations are common when the Holy Spirit brings His anointing.

Jesus said the anointing breaks the yoke (Isaiah 10:27, KJV) and sets the captives free (61:1). A recent example happened in our downtown healing room. Teresa came into Hope City, an inner-city ministry where we have a healing room, primarily for something to eat. She was in a motorized wheelchair so she obviously had some physical handicap. We asked if we could pray for her, and she wheeled herself into the prayer room. She said for eight years she had struggled with a bone condition that caused her bones to deteriorate. She was in a great deal of pain throughout her body, had pulmonary problems, and was confined to her wheelchair. As we began to pray for her, the anointing came on her and she began to shake and vibrate. We had witnessed such manifestations before but didn't know if she had. We asked if she was afraid and she said, "No, this is the Lord. I've never felt Him like this before, but it's the Lord." As we continued to pray, she started to take deep breaths. Soon she said, "The brick that was in my chest is gone. I can breathe." Doris asked if she had pulmonary problems, and she said that she usually was on oxygen but the tank was so painful for her to lift and bring with her that she just left it home. Then she began to lift her arms. "He's given me my arms back," she said. A little later she was moving her feet. Doris asked her if she could do that before, and she said no. We were so excited about what God was doing with Teresa that I brought a couple of others into the healing room so they could witness a miracle in process. It was soon time for the evening group meeting, so we quit praying for Teresa in the healing room and moved to the larger prayer room. Teresa was asked to share her testimony at the group meeting; and after she did, ministry was offered to others needing healing. A few people from the group joined us as we prayed some more for Teresa after she shared her healing testimony. As we prayed for her, she began moving her feet in circles and declared that she wanted to get up and walk. She then stood up from her wheelchair and began to slowly walk across the room. We were all excited to see what God was doing with her. It was not an issue that she was moving slowly as we knew that having been in a wheelchair for so long, her muscles would likely have weakened and would need to be used to become strong once again. She rested for awhile, then walked some more before finally sitting back down in her motorized chair for her trip home. We praise God for his grace and love.

Several scriptures confirm the supernatural anointing for exploits when the Spirit comes upon someone. Some examples are:

When the Spirit came *upon* (clothed) Gideon (Judges 6:34)

When the Spirit of the Lord came *upon* (rushed upon) Sampson (Judges 14:6)

When Jesus was conceived by the Holy Spirit, the angel told Mary that the Holy Spirit would come *upon* her (Luke 1:35)

Jesus told His disciples that they would receive power when the Holy Spirit came *upon* them (Acts 1:8)

There is a connection between these last two examples; the language Luke uses is very similar and both express power when God comes to live in man, both Jesus and the Holy Spirit being recognized as God.

Anointing in Jesus' Earthly Life

The Holy Spirit and power are linked together; they cannot be separated. We see this in the life of Jesus. He laid down His divine attributes and set an example for us of how a sinless Man, one totally devoted to the Father and under the anointing of the Spirit, can function here on earth. Acts 10:38 tells us that Jesus was anointed with the Holy Spirit and with power and how the outcome of this anointing was His ability to do good and to heal all who were oppressed by the devil. We too can do good and heal the oppressed under the anointing of the Spirit.

Under the authority of the Father, the anointing allowed Jesus to heal all those who came to Him for healing. In Luke 5:17 and Luke 6:19, we can see that power was present for healing and He healed them all.

When the anointing is present for healing, healing becomes easy. We have seen several people who could not lift their arms very high, due to injury or surgery, begin to wave their arms overhead without pain after a brief prayer under the anointing of God. Under the anointing I once ran my fingers over a woman's crooked finger and it was immediately straightened. Recently we had a woman with colon cancer come into the healing room. She was an indigent without financial resources for medical treatment but had been diagnosed with cancer at a local hospital. As we briefly prayed for her, the power of God hit her body and she began to shake and vibrate violently to the point that she had difficulty staying upright in her chair. She declared, "I feel good!" The pain in her abdomen was gone. This lady searched me out a day later to let me know that she still "felt good." Was she healed? I presume so, she certainly thought she was. We may not see her again until we meet in heaven.

How Can We Position Ourselves to Receive the Anointing?

First of all, we recognize that the anointing is from God. We can't make it happen, but we can search out scriptural principles that position us to receive and flow in His anointing. As I have sought the anointing to heal the sick, I've found the guidelines listed below to be helpful.

1. Ask: Ephesians 3:20 tells us that God is able to do far more than we can ask or even think. Jesus also encouraged us to ask. In Luke 11:9-13 He said to ask, seek, and knock and we would receive and find and the doors would be opened. The Greek here for the word *ask* actually means a continuous asking; so, ask and keep asking until you receive. Don't ask for healing just once, keep asking. Keep asking for the anointing; be hungry to receive it. God promises to satisfy those who hunger and thirst for righteousness (Matthew 5:6). We ask based on our relationship with the Lord and our trust in Him; He can do what He said He will do. The parable of the wise and foolish virgins (Matthew 25:1-13) illustrates how important it is to be in constant relationship with the Lord. This parable is given to the church; all the virgins were waiting for the bridegroom (Jesus). They were all believers. The oil, which is a type of the Holy Spirit, cannot be passed from one believer to another; the source is Jesus. Maintain a fresh relationship with the One who supplies His Spirit to us.

2. Prayer: Jesus is our example; He spent a great deal of time in prayer. The examples in Luke cited above illustrate how key prayer was with regard to power being present to heal the sick. In Luke 5:17 where "*the power of the Lord was present for Him to perform healing*," the previous verse indicates that Jesus often slipped away by Himself to pray. Again, in Luke 6:19 where "*power was coming from Him and healing them all*," this healing event follows a time He went off to the mountain to spend the night in prayer to God (v. 12). By God's grace, I've maintained a personal prayer time for over thirty-five years. It has changed my life.

3. Pray in tongues: Praying in tongues is often the entry door into the things of the Spirit; it was for me. It's available to Christians through the baptism with the Holy Spirit (Acts 1:5; Matthew 3:11). The baptism with the Holy Spirit is one of the few things mentioned in each of the four Gospels; this emphasizes its importance. Paul said that he spoke in tongues more than others did (1 Corinthians 14:18) and he wished that we all would speak in tongues (v. 5). If speaking in tongues was something that Paul stressed, it should be something we pay close attention to as well. For, after all:

> God performed extraordinary miracles through Paul (Acts 19:11). Paul received direct revelation from Jesus Christ (Galatians 1:11-12). Paul was able to shake off an attack of the enemy without damage (Acts 28:1-5).

We've seen a few extraordinary miracles. One such miracle was the restoration of Anthony's foot that was shared in chapter 1. Kevin Basconi shares some of the revelation he has received from his visits to heaven in his trilogy of books on *Dancing with Angels*.[2] Kevin credits much of his supernatural experiences to the time he spends praying in tongues. Tongues is one of the most maligned and misunderstood gifts from God.

4. Obedience to God: Acts 5:32 states that the Holy Spirit is given to those that obey Him. This is only common sense. Why would God give the anointing of the Spirit to someone who was not following the leading

---

2   Kevin Basconi, *Dancing with Angels*, Book 1, and *Angels in the Realms of Heaven*, Book 2 (Shippensburg, PA: Destiny Image Publishers, 2010 and 2012).

of the Spirit? Suppose I have the choice of staying at home to watch the midsummer all-star baseball game on TV or of going to the healing rooms to pray for the sick. Staying home to watch the game is not evil, but I would not expect the anointing of the Spirit as I watch the game. However, I will need the anointing if I go to minister in the healing rooms. In 1974 my wife and I were still members of a traditional denominational church and were living in Blacksburg, Virginia, where I was an Assistant Professor of Civil Engineering at Virginia Polytechnic and State University. We had not heard of the baptism with the Holy Spirit and were not even familiar with the term "charismatic." Yet, we were serious Christians and did have a desire to follow the Lord. When presented with an unsolicited opportunity to move to South Dakota and teach there, we sought the Lord but couldn't seem to discern what we should do. Then He spoke to us; not exactly in an external audible voice but in a loud internal voice that neither of us could deny. We knew we were to move to South Dakota even though it seemed like a foolish decision from a professional standpoint. We made the move, and God not only blessed my professional career but led us into the baptism of the Holy Spirit as well. I wasn't aware of the implied promise in Acts 5:32, but God knew it was there. I sometimes wonder if He felt He needed to give us the opportunity to be baptized in the Holy Spirit because we were obedient and made the decision to move to South Dakota.

5. Humility: First Peter 5:5-6 indicates the importance of being humble; it even says that God opposes the proud. Life and ministry are difficult enough without being opposed by God! But what does it mean to be humble? Jesus was humble; He humbled Himself and was obedient to the Father's will (Philippians 2:8; Matthew 26:39), and yet He was not some kind of anemic weak person. Humility is about being transparent with others and not pretending to be someone we aren't. Humility is also accepting what God says about you, personally and through His Word. There are many scriptures that define who we are in Christ, and we need to agree with them. One difficult area is how to share testimonies without drawing undue attention to yourself while giving honor to the Lord for what He has done. For example, in India we prayed with a young man who had been stabbed with a sword as he made a decision to leave his gang after accepting Jesus. His shoulder was badly damaged and the Lord instantly healed it. A safeguard in these situations is to pray in teams, which we were doing. Then no one person is likely to become puffed up because of a healing. We stress Matthew 5:16. We try to have the attitude in doing things *"in such a way"* that when men see the good work they give glory to our heavenly Father.

6. Study the Word: We must spend time in God's Word; it reveals His plan for us as well as how He relates to people. Study helps position us so He can trust us with the anointing. Romans 1:16 says that the gospel *"is the power of God for salvation to everyone who believes."* Thus it supplies power for salvation from sin, salvation from demonic oppression, and salvation from sickness and disease. What does the gospel mean to you? If asked, could you give a short account of it? We need to be able to do this.

7. Be in spiritual fellowship with other believers: The Bible tells us that we should not forget to assemble together with other Christians (Hebrews 10:25). We should be under the covering of a local pastor and congregation. It allows other spiritual people to speak into our lives and helps keep us from error. It also gives us some protection from the evil one as he seeks to discredit all who are striving to further the kingdom of God. Problems in marriage and ministries are all too common for those that neglect this admonition. Currently there is a trend in this digital age to join a church broadcasting on the web. This approach is understandable and perhaps necessary for homebound individuals or people living in a repressive society where Christianity is not allowed. For Western believers this trend may be good or not; we will let history be the judge. Obviously, teaching can be received via the web and tithes transferred as God directs. However, there is the danger that the viewer is not accountable to any spiritual authority; and certainly there is not the opportunity to minister love and encouragement with a timely word or hug to another believer, let alone lay hands on the sick or enjoy the joys of worshiping Jesus in a corporate environment.

8. Get to know Jesus: There is so much to know about the Lord that we will need eternity to accomplish this task. But it is to our advantage to get started on this journey here on earth. John 17:3 tells us that eternal life is knowing Jesus and the Father who sent Him. Paul knew the importance of this activity as he often prayed that Christians would increase in the knowledge of God (Colossians 1:9-10). We know that Christ lives in us; and as Doris likes to say, "We are His ride." Let's take Him on some adventures!

CHAPTER 4

Using the Word of Knowledge in Healing

What is a word of knowledge? Paul lists this gift with the nine supernatural gifts of the Holy Spirit that he mentions in chapter 12 of 1 Corinthians. In verses 7-8, Paul writes; *"But to each one is given the manifestation of the Spirit for the common good. For to one is given the word of wisdom through the Spirit, and to another the word of knowledge according to the same Spirit."* Notice that the word of knowledge is a supernatural gift from the Holy Spirit, not from an evil or familiar spirit. This is a good gift. In fact, verse 7 indicates that it is given *"for the common good."* It is not given to glorify some human vessel, instead it is given to help accomplish God's purpose at that particular moment.

Some believe that a word of knowledge is primarily connected with special revelation to help with teaching the scriptures. I personally believe it is much more than that, and I concur with John Wimber who taught that a word of knowledge is the supernatural revelation of facts about a person or situation which is not learned through the efforts of the natural minds, but is a fragment of knowledge freely given by God, disclosing the truth which the Spirit wishes to be made known concerning a particular person or situation.

Imagine an enormous library where, somehow, all the details of the lives of every single human being that was alive on the earth were gathered; and there was a book in this library that corresponded to each individual.

God knows all this information; each person's life is an open book before Him. Then at a particular instant and for purposes and timing that only He knows, He chooses to reveal one word of this information to one of His servants. It is not a page, a paragraph, or a sentence from this book; it is only a word. One little bit of information out of His vast understanding and knowledge. It can be more than a single word, obviously, but many times it is only that. The Lord reveals "heart" or "ear," etc., and the one receiving the word must wrestle with what he has heard and how it is to be used.

The word of knowledge can be extremely useful in many situations, and it is often given to initiate the healing process. A small group may have gathered for prayer, for example, and while praying one member of the group is impressed that someone in the group is suffering from back pain. After carefully considering whether this is a prompting from the Holy Spirit or not, the word is shared within the group and someone may respond that they are experiencing pain in their back. Then all would minister to the individual with the pain having the expectation that the situation would be remedied because the Lord brought forth the information.

Why Does God Reveal Information Through the Word of Knowledge?

First of all, a word of knowledge reveals to us that God is an all-knowing, supernatural God. This fact is at the very center of Christianity. That God chooses to reveal part of His knowledge to Christians illustrates His commitment to use the church as a vehicle to accomplish His will on earth as well as His desire to love and bless us all. He has entrusted us with the gospel, has commissioned us to spread it, and has committed Himself to help us with our tasks. The word of knowledge is one such way that help is given.

The word of knowledge also emphasizes, what we already know, that God knows all about us. A friend of ours had quit pastoring his church and moved his family to Oklahoma to receive some mission training. It was a difficult time for him, and at one point he was quite discouraged with his situation. He felt deserted by the Lord and remembers telling the Lord that he didn't think that God even knew where he lived anymore. Soon thereafter he attended a midweek church service where a visiting minister delivered the sermon. Shortly after the minister began to speak, he paused, pointed his finger at our friend, told him to stand, and said: "Young man, God does know where you live! He knows your address and your telephone number and everything about you!" Our friend was overcome by the Spirit right where he was sitting. He missed hearing the sermon but went home to his family an encouraged man. He later was used by the Lord in a powerful way to spread the gospel and heal the sick in the Far East.

We must remember that the word of knowledge is a spiritual tool for *use* in a spiritual world. Tools are to be used not admired. I wouldn't think of inviting you to my house to show off a set of screwdrivers or wrenches that I kept polished and clean in my garage. You would want to know why I had them if I never used them. In this same way, the spiritual gifts, including the word of knowledge, are given by God to be used, not admired.

I think another reason that God sends the word of knowledge so frequently is that He wants to make believers out of us. Most of us in the church can identify with the father of the epileptic son who cried out and said, "I do believe; help my unbelief" (Mark 9:24). Jesus promised us that if we could just believe in Him, we could do the works that He did (John 14:12). We can't make that kind of pure and total belief in Jesus happen by ourselves. Seeing the good that comes from the application of the word of knowledge helps us along the path of belief.

How Does the Word of Knowledge Happen?

Because one person is different from another, the Lord communicates with His people in different ways. So the way He conveys a word of knowledge to me may be different than the way He does to you. However, it's always helpful to learn how God works out things in someone else's life as an indicator of how He might choose to work in yours.

In John 10:4 Jesus says that sheep will follow the shepherd because they know His voice. It's that way with us as we begin to discern the voice of the Spirit from our own thoughts or desires. I don't think anyone has this perfected yet, and as humans we are subject to making a mistake; but the more we listen and learn, the better we get at knowing when we are receiving a word from the Lord. For me, the purest words of knowledge normally come when my attention is focused on the Lord. This can be when I'm praying or possibly during worship on a Sunday morning.

I remember one time when I was to help my friend Jim Goll teach a class on healing at the Grace Training Center. Jim ministers full time, and you may be familiar with him as he travels and ministers internationally in addition to being the author of several publications and books. Jim specifically wanted me to address the subject of using words of knowledge. As I was praying about the class, an image of a young woman came into my mind with the thought that she had suffered a neck injury and it still was a problem for her. I remembered seeing this woman at a recent service; but I did not know if she was a member of Jim's class or if she had any problem with her neck. That evening as I sat in the classroom waiting for Jim to start the class, I looked around for this particular woman; but she was nowhere to be seen. Then, just before the class was to begin, she hurried in and took a seat. When my turn came to begin my teaching, I asked her if she had a problem with her neck. Indeed she did! She had been in a car accident in California and had received a neck injury that still gave her a lot of difficulty. I asked her to come forward for prayer, and several of those in the class also came up to help me pray for her. I was very thankful that I knew it was the Lord's idea and not mine because her head started whipping rapidly back and forth as we prayed. She was not totally healed on the spot, but experienced a significant improvement and her neck was gradually healed as I and others prayed for her on several occasions after that. Praise the Lord!

Many times during worship before a church service begins, I will receive a word, or words, of knowledge regarding healing. One weekend when Doris and I were on a ministry trip with Jim Goll to Detroit, I had a word of knowledge about someone who had a sore on their upper arm. I shared this with the group and later found out that I had unknowingly pointed to a spot on my arm that was exactly where a young man had an ugly sore. He responded to the word and told us that he had been bitten on his upper arm when he had intervened in an altercation several weeks ago. He rolled up his sleeve to show us his arm. It was a nasty looking sore that covered several inches of his upper arm. We simply prayed and asked the Lord for healing, and the next day he showed us all that overnight it had almost completely disappeared. God is so good to us to allow us to take part in these events.

It is also very common to receive a word of knowledge *as* you are ministering to someone, not just *before* you minister. This is actually the most common way for most of us. I believe that the Lord wants to minister to His people even more than we do, and we get the words to help us along the way after we have already committed to do the ministry. A case in point is when a member of our congregation asked me to pray for his knee. As I prayed for his knee, the Lord shared some information with me regarding his unsaved brother. We ended up praying for the brother too. I'm not sure of the end result regarding the brother's salvation, but I know my friend was encouraged just knowing that it was on God's heart. He knew that God had heard his prayers for his brother. What more can we ask?

Although it happens infrequently, the Lord sometimes interrupts my daily activities and gives me a word of knowledge. One of the more dramatic times this happened was when I was driving down a lonely highway in South Dakota. Doris and I were preparing to go to Minneapolis the next weekend to give a healing workshop at a Francis MacNutt seminar. Francis is a former Catholic priest who has an extensive physical and emotional healing ministry based in Jacksonville, Florida. As I drove, I "saw" people in the class we would have, where they were sitting, and what they would be wearing. As I remember, my attention was drawn to four different individuals and I knew that I was to minister to them on some specific topics after the class. Imagine my relief when I spotted them at our workshop, sitting where I had seen them and wearing the correct clothes. I correctly identified three of the four, although I was somewhat confused on the fourth and never will know if I did that one properly. It certainly gave me, as well as them, confidence that they were in the right spot that day.

Although most of my words of knowledge are audio and come through my thoughts, others receive information from the Lord in different ways. Some see pictures and others may feel pain in their bodies. I often chuckle when I see Jim Goll praying for someone and his head is rotating back and forth as he prays. It's almost a sure bet that he is seeing in the spirit and is actually reading what he is seeing over the head of the person to whom he is ministering. God is a God of variety, and I encourage you to explore how He wants to communicate with you.

Possible Outcomes

Whenever a word of knowledge is given for healing, one of three possible things will happen:

1. The person for whom the word was intended (by God) will respond, receive ministry, and the word will be fulfilled; i.e., the healing will occur.
2. The person for whom the word was intended will respond, they will receive ministry, but the healing does not occur.
3. The person for whom the word was intended does not respond, so the healing does not happen.

In any of the three outcomes listed above, someone else, besides the person for whom the word was intended, may respond and they may or may not receive healing. I don't get too concerned about this. Our place is to give the word to the best of our ability and then minister to those who come forward. Even if we know the person(s) who responds does not fit the specifics of the word of knowledge, pray for them anyway. We have been commissioned to heal the sick (Mark 16:18) whenever and wherever we find them, not only when preceded by a word of knowledge. Let's look more closely at each of these three outcomes.

1. The person responds and the healing comes.

This, indeed, is the goal of both the one ministering and the person coming forward for ministry. We praise God for this operation of the Spirit and the good fruit that we have seen from it. God is faithful and we have seen this outcome happen time and time again. I will share just one small example here:

> One Sunday I was ministering the word at an evening service for a small fellowship in Rapid City, South Dakota. Joy Church was in its beginning stages and occupied a rented meeting room in the Civic Center on Sundays. That Sunday evening the gathering was very modest, consisting of approximately forty people. During the

service, a young man came in and took a seat in the very back, far away from the rest of those in attendance. He was obviously down on his luck, appeared to be living on the street, and we presumed he came into the meeting to just get warm as it was quite cold outside.

At the end of the service, I had a word of knowledge about someone having a sore foot. I gave the word, but no one in the congregation responded to it. Being fairly certain that I had indeed heard the Lord, I waited for a few minutes and then asked again if anyone had a sore foot. Clear in the back, the young man raised his hand and said, "I've got a sore foot." I encouraged him to come forward for prayer as I believed that God wanted to heal him. As he swaggered forward, I could almost hear his thoughts, "What kind of nonsense is this?" Nevertheless, he did allow us to pray for him and then he immediately left the room before we could share the Lord any further. We later found out that he had gone directly into a restroom and removed his sock and shoe and examined his foot. It was already healed with new flesh where previously he had some sores. Brian has struggled with the Lord since that time, over thirty years ago. He has been up and down, in and out of church, and in and out of our lives. We last received a call from him several years ago. He still hadn't completely turned his life over to the Lord (have any of us?); but he wanted us to know that he had rededicated his life to God and was back in church. He said from that very first night when he saw his foot healed through prayer, "I know there is a God."

2. The person responds but the healing doesn't happen.

Unfortunately, this outcome is quite common. I used to think that if I got a word of knowledge correct, that the healing would automatically occur. I don't think that anymore; in fact, there are several reasons why the healing may not happen.

There may be some difficulty or hindrance in the person receiving the ministry or in the one doing the ministry. I am so accustomed to the Lord giving me words of knowledge for healing that I almost always just automatically assume that any word which identifies a person's illness was given so they could be healed. That is not always the case. There are times when the word is given so that the person can be identified for some other reason.

For example, one Sunday morning I received a word about a man who was suffering from depression. I thought the man did not regularly attend Metro Christian Fellowship (MCF) and that he was about fifty-two years old. I gave the word at the close of the service, but nobody responded to it. During the ministry time after the service, a young man from our congregation brought up a visitor for prayer. The young man told me that he thought that his visitor fit the word of knowledge, so we dialoged with the visitor for a time. It was his first time at MCF, he was fifty-two, and had been seeing a psychiatrist for depression. I told him that I thought he fit the word of knowledge pretty well and we prayed for his depression to lift. I also found out that he was not a believer so we made an appointment to discuss what being a Christian is all about. I saw this man several times but he never accepted Jesus as his Lord because he just could not accept the fact that Jesus would not want him to participate in certain kinds of sin. In retrospect, I believe that the initial word of knowledge was to identify this man as a candidate for salvation, not just for healing of the depression. God is concerned about our bodies but his first priority is our souls.

I also believe that we can offend the Holy Spirit and that sometimes He simply withdraws and the healing doesn't happen. The Holy Spirit is not timid and He will doggedly pursue accomplishing God's will, but we must remember to treat Him with respect. He is God and is deserving of our honor and attention. If we are rude or disrespectful when He is ministering, He may decide to do the healing some other time.

We can also expect Satan, our enemy, to resist the healing. In these cases, we need to be assured that we are acting in accord with the Father's will and we need to ask for the grace to not quit. Persistence is frequently lacking in all areas of the current generation. We have been raised on television episodes that were always completed by the beginning of the next show. It doesn't work that easily in real life. In Romans 5 Paul writes that tribulation should bring perseverance and that the perseverance will help develop our character and bring us the hope we need. God wants us to learn to have faith in Him and to persevere until His answer comes. That was Daniel's strategy in Daniel 9 and 10. We find that although God sent the answer to

Daniel's prayers immediately, it took three weeks for the answer to arrive because of Satan's hindrances.

There are undoubtedly other reasons why the healing doesn't always come when a person responds to a word of knowledge, but I'm not smart enough to know exactly what they are. Frankly, sometimes I just don't know why the healing doesn't come. We have some people we know that have struggled with their illnesses for years. They are faithful people, devoted to the Lord, and yet their healing doesn't come. I have prayed for several of these people many times, and I have seen visiting ministers receive words of knowledge concerning them and call them out of large crowds for their healing—yet they still have the illness. We live in that in-between time, the time when Jesus said the Father has chosen to give us the kingdom (Luke 12:32) but it has obviously not fully arrived.

3. The person doesn't respond.

Frequently when a person does not respond to a word of knowledge it is because they are unfamiliar with this activity of the Spirit and they do not know what is expected of them. They may be afraid to respond publicly, they may not believe that God gives words of knowledge or heals today, they may misunderstand the word, or they may think it must be for someone else. In these situations, it is necessary for the one giving the word to be patient and to repeat the word again. Being patient allows the recipient time to consider if they should respond and repeating the word allows them to rethink what was said and whether they might be the one for whom the word is intended. People may not be used to responding or perhaps they were not paying close attention when the word was given. Patience and repeating the word are the best tools here. However, we must be careful to not coax or manipulate someone into responding.

The one giving the word should also make it a habit to ask the Lord to grace him or her with more specific words of knowledge. The more details that can be given about a particular person or situation, the more likely it is that a person will respond. People are naturally reluctant to identify themselves, and the additional details encourage them that God has really identified their particular illness. It is not uncommon to give a word of knowledge, not have anyone respond, and then be approached after the meeting by someone who matches the word exactly. Sometimes, I think, this is actually God's design as it tends to keep us humble when we give words in public for which there seemingly is no response.

One Sunday morning I had a word of knowledge for a woman at our first service visiting from outside the Kansas City area who was about thirty-nine years old and had a persistent ringing in her left ear. A woman visiting from South Dakota responded to the word and everything was accurate except the ringing was in her right ear instead of her left one. The different facets of this word along with the actual situation are detailed in Table 1. The point of making this comparison is that even though it was a very detailed and accurate word, it still was not 100 percent correct. We are all human and God's information comes through our human filter. Thus, both the giver and the receiver of words of knowledge need to take this into consideration.

Table 1: Word of Knowledge Comparison

Word	Actual
Woman	Yes
Attending first service	Yes
Lived outside of Kansas City	Yes, from Sturgis, SD
About thirty-nine years old	Yes, forty years old
Persistent ringing	Yes, for twenty years
Left ear	No, right ear

And finally, the person giving the word of knowledge may be the reason that no one responds. The word may have not been communicated clearly, and we need to be alert to ineffective communication and learn to express ourselves explicitly. We also may have missed God and the word was not a true word from Him at all. This has happened to me several times; but as we continue to step out, our past experiences will help us here immensely. Above all, give any word that you honestly feel is from the Lord. Even if no one responds, it is far better that you look a little foolish in front of people than to go home with a blessing for someone that they did not receive because you were afraid to give the word of knowledge.

CHAPTER 5

Healing Models

In this chapter we will explore some ways to minister healing. Models are a framework for ministry; they are not meant to be followed rigidly but do provide a way to begin ministering to someone. Always seek and follow the leading of the Spirit whenever praying for the sick. The models presented here are based on years of experience of ministering to the sick.

Happy Hunter's Healing Model

Charles and Frances Hunter were our favorite healing evangelists. They have gone on to be with the Lord and receive their heavenly rewards, which I'm sure are substantial. We appreciated the Hunter's desire to see the sick healed and the lost saved. They also were willing to travel wherever God was sending them and at their own expense. Their only financial request was to receive a love offering; they paid their own way out of that. Only the Lord knows how many received the baptism with the Holy Spirit, how many sick were healed, and the number of unbelievers converted during their earthly ministry. Doris and I have tried to model our ministry after theirs, and we've never lacked for the resources to travel to meetings and accommodate other expenses.

We have witnessed many miracles and healings when observing those ministered to by Charles and Frances. One of our first encounters with them occurred in the late '70s in Sioux Falls, South Dakota. At a meeting there Frances had a word of knowledge regarding someone with scleroderma, a disease that causes the skin and organs to thicken and harden. It eventually develops a shiny, wax like appearance along with other symptoms. A lady stood to her feet to acknowledge that she had scleroderma; it happened that she was near where I was sitting and her condition was very obvious. Frances simply declared the healing from the stage; the woman fell under the power of the Spirit and rested on the floor at her seat. It was wonderful to watch her skin change consistency right before our eyes; what a marvelous healing!

We received some valuable teaching regarding praying for the sick from the Hunters, although they would not agree with my terminology of "praying" for the sick. They correctly pointed out that Jesus never prayed for the sick; He just healed them and sent out His disciples to do the same. Luke records that in Luke 9:1-2:

> *He called the twelve together, and gave them power and authority over all the demons and to heal diseases. And He sent them out to proclaim the kingdom of God and to heal diseases.*

He did not tell them to pray for the sick; they were just to heal them. This information has affected the way we minister to the sick in that we often command organs to respond, the sickness to leave, etc. We don't get too rigid in our approach, however. Remember that Jesus also invited us to ask Him and He would do it, as long as we asked in His name (John 14:14). Asking in His name implies something more than just a few words tacked onto the end of a prayer, but we will not go into detail about that here.

One thing the Hunters stressed was that spirits are often involved in keeping someone ill. Even if a demonic entity is not the source of the illness, it may take advantage of the situation to hinder a person receiving healing from the Lord. As mentioned previously, in Luke 13:11 we see an example of Jesus healing someone after He dispatched the hindering spirit first. It is clear from the scripture that the woman's sickness was caused by an evil spirit. Jesus first freed her from the spirit (v. 12) and then laid his hands on her for healing. We have seen this scenario repeated over and over in our own ministry. An example of this type of healing was when we ministered to Terry, an asthmatic sufferer. We first took authority over a spirit of asthma and removed it and then prayed for healing. Terry happened to have a doctor's appointment the day after we ministered to her. She felt so much better after receiving prayer that her doctor did some testing. They found that overnight her lung capacity had improved from 33 percent to almost 100 percent. In addition, Terry said that TMJ issues with her jaw were no longer a problem. God is so good!

The Hunter's model centers on adjusting body parts to remove pain and bring healing. Our bodies rely on muscles, tendons, and ligaments to hold our frame in place. Many times our skeleton gets slightly out of place and it causes pressure on nerves or organs which results in pain in various locations. They teach to lay hands on four different locations and then command adjustment to occur in the name of Jesus. These four locations are:

1. The ankles for adjustment of the back muscles and legs
2. The hips for adjustment of the pelvis area
3. The arms for adjustment of the upper spinal column
4. The neck for adjustment of the higher vertebra and discs

Let's examine how to adjust these four locations in greater detail as so many people in the world have back problems, headaches, kidney issues, intestinal disorders, etc. Many times simply adjusting one or all of these areas solves the problem. It is important to stress that the minister does not push or pull on a body part or attempt to do any of the adjustments on his own. Any adjustment of body parts occurs by the Holy Spirit.

1. Adjusting the Legs: The person with the lower back pain should sit in a straight chair and extend their legs so the minister is able to place his thumbs on the ankle bone. When we first started doing this adjustment, we tried to line up the heels of the feet, but Charles Hunter was the one who taught us to use the ankles. That technique is less susceptible to error. Often the thumbs will not meet, in other words they will not appear to be the same distance from the waist on each leg and one leg will appear to be shorter than the other. Unless there has been an injury or surgery of some kind, everyone is created by God with two legs that are the same distance from their hip joint to their ankle. If the thumbs do not meet, it normally means the back muscles have drawn one leg up slightly or the spine is out of alignment so the leg appears to be short. At this point, the one ministering simply commands the back muscles to relax and the leg to come to its proper position. It will then move into position and the thumbs will now meet. We have done this simple procedure with good results hundreds, if not thousands of times over the years. It is always fun to do and we encourage people to keep their eyes open and watch the thumbs move as the leg comes into place. Many times the person being ministered to also feels their leg move in addition to watching the thumbs move. Some people don't understand why the body should respond when we make this command; but why not? We have the faith for this. Jesus said if we had sufficient faith even mountains would move at our command. The first time I did this adjustment, I was very tentative and unsure about what would happen. The leg came down, the pain left, and my confidence grew. Now, every time we do this adjustment, it always happens. No exceptions.

So many people around the world have back pain. When we minister in India, a line forms at the chair we are using as almost all of them have back pain from carrying heavy loads on their heads. At our first meeting in Mumbai, I did this procedure on Willie, not knowing that he actually had a short leg due to a previous injury. When Willie walked into the meeting the next day, the local pastors were amazed as he no longer walked with a limp. They still refer to this miracle of healing as "Willie's miracle." In this case God actually did a creative miracle of healing; I just thought his back was being adjusted. We have many testimonies that confirm the success of this method. Diane shares a common story: She had been having back pain for several weeks. The doctor told her she had one leg one inch shorter than the other and that her whole frame was tilted. After prayer, not only was the pain gone but when her doctor rechecked her, he said she was no longer misaligned.

2. Adjusting the Pelvic Area: We almost always do this adjustment in conjunction with adjusting the legs as frequently both the legs and pelvis adjustment are needed to achieve relief from lower back pain. In this adjustment, the minister or the recipient lays his hands on the hips and commands the pelvis to come into proper position. It is important to be sensitive to the one receiving ministry. While a man is normally comfortable with another man placing his hands on his hips, for example, it would be improper for a man to lay his hands on a woman's hips. Effective results are still obtained if a lady places her hands on her hips and the minister lays his hands on top of hers. After the command is given for the pelvis to come into position, it will usually begin to rotate slightly from side to side. Sometimes this rotation is slight, and sometimes it is more extensive. Neither the minister nor the ministry recipient causes the motion. Whether it is an angel, the Holy Spirit, or the Lord Himself doing the adjustment, I don't know. I do know it happens, heaven causes it to happen, and it is very effective. When doing this adjustment, I always keep my touch on the hips very light, sometimes using only a finger or two on each hip. That way the person receiving ministry knows you are not causing the rotation. We are in relationship with a Lutheran pastor who refers to this adjustment as the "washing machine prayer."

3. Adjusting the Arms: Upper back pain is often caused by misalignment of the spinal column. Scoliosis is one of the serious infirmities that can cause upper back pain. We refer to this adjustment as "adjusting the arms"; but just as the legs are normally of the same length, the arms are as well. God knows how to create limbs of equal length. As with the legs, muscles, ligaments, tendons, discs, and vertebra can cause one arm to appear shorter than the other. To measure we have the person receiving ministry stand with their toes together and swing their arms wide and bring them together stretched as far as they can to see if the finger tips on each hand match up. If one arm appears shorter than the other, we simply command the back to relax and the arm to come into proper position. This command can be issued while touching the hands or not, depending upon the minister's preference. I normally like to gently place my hands beneath the recipient's hands as a means of having a contact point but have sometimes commanded them to move without touching them as a demonstration of the power embedded within the name of Jesus. Even if the fingertips match each other, we usually still command the upper back to be adjusted. Frequently the arms will begin to repeatedly move in and out as the upper back comes into adjustment. I'm not exactly sure what is happening, but it appears that the Spirit is working His way up the spinal column disc by disc, vertebra by vertebra. When the ministry teams prayed over Darla's arms, she could feel and hear bones moving in her back. She had been suffering with upper back pain but was pain free after ministry.

4. Adjusting the Neck: Again, when adjusting the neck, take care not to initiate any movement yourself; let the Lord direct it. Place one hand gently on the base of the neck and gently hold the cheek of the individual with the other. Command body parts to be in the proper position. As you do this, the head will often slowly rotate or move as the adjustment is made. Frequently as the adjustment nears completion, the head will begin to tip to the rear. People with neck pain or frequent headaches often will receive permanent relief when ministered to in this manner. Kyle was a young man who suffered from debilitating migraine headaches. He became totally free from this infirmity after receiving the ministry described here.

We recently conducted a training session for people involved in opening a new healing room. We called a friend up to use as a model as we demonstrated adjusting legs, pelvis, arms, and neck. We were just using her to demonstrate the model and did not know she had scoliosis. As we demonstrated, her body began moving and twisting under the power of God. We later learned that her scoliosis was healed and she is now taller than before.

Remember that Jesus said the sick would recover when they had hands laid on them (Mark 16:18). He did not say that everyone we minister to would be instantly healed. We like instant healings, pain being gone, etc.; but many healings we see are a process and the healing may take a few hours or a few days to be completed. This should not discourage us. If someone has endured pain in their body for several years, why should we be upset if it takes a day or two for the healing to come? One thing to remember then is not to consider the prayer time as ineffective if the one receiving ministry does not receive an instant healing. I remember praying one Sunday after the morning service for Kevin. He had injured his back and was having difficulty sitting or walking because of back pain. He did not feel any difference after I prayed for him, but by evening he was playing basketball without pain.

Vineyard's Five Step Healing Model

John Wimber taught a healing model that was developed while he was leading the Vineyard. It consists of:

1. The Interview

2. The Diagnostic Decision
3. Prayer Selection
4. Prayer Engagement
5. Post Prayer Direction

1. The Interview: The interview is a naturally the first step in ministering to someone; it simply is finding out why they want prayer. It is not meant to be a medical interview where the ministry team receives medical data, etc., but the person coming for prayer will often offer some medical information such as my blood pressure is too high, or my leg was broken in a car accident. While listening to the condition being described, the team needs to also listen for supernatural revelation from the Holy Spirit. For instance, someone may want prayer for injuries sustained in an automobile accident. The Holy Spirit prompts some additional questioning and it is discovered that the individual has been involved in six auto accidents in the last two years. Obviously this is not normal and some spiritual issues will also probably need to be addressed. The team does need to pray intelligently, so the interview is important; but it should be kept brief.

2. Diagnostic Decision: After the interview, the ministry team needs to decide if the problem is strictly physical in nature or if some spiritual issues are also involved and then pray accordingly. Seek for answers to the questions, why does this person have this problem? And, is the problem caused by a natural occurrence such as an injury or disease or is there demonic activity involved? Sometimes both areas need to be addressed for the healing to manifest. There may be a hindering spirit, for instance, which should be removed prior to ministering physical healing. We once were asked to minister to a young woman in a wheelchair after a conference we attended. For some time several people had been praying for her without any apparent success. As we began to pray for her, the Holy Spirit prompted me to ask some details about her situation. She indicated that she had surgery for a head injury, which was expected to proceed without complications. Unfortunately, the surgeon had a major mishap during surgery and it left her a quadriplegic, without use of either arms or legs. It is understandable that the wheelchair bound young woman would have intense feelings about the doctor who performed her surgery. As we inquired about unforgiveness toward him, it became obvious that this was a major matter of concern. As we shared the importance of forgiveness for others, especially this physician, she understood that not forgiving him was hindering her relationship with the Lord. As she made the decision to forgive the surgeon, suddenly her left arm began to vibrate and she regained motion in that arm; no one was praying for her at the time. We were excited and had high expectation that she could receive additional healing, but the hour was late and the people who brought her to the conference were anxious to leave so the ministry time was terminated. We hoped to have the opportunity to minister to her further at some future time but that did not happen.

3. Prayer Selection: The ministry team must now select how to minister. In general there are two main categories of prayer; prayer toward God and prayer from God. In prayer toward God we are employing either petition, asking God to do the healing, or we initiate a prayer of intercession of behalf of the one seeking healing. Even though Jesus commanded healing to come and didn't petition God to do the healing, petition is valid as He invited us to ask expectantly (John 14:13-14; Luke 11:9-10). An example of this type of prayer can be found in Mark 10:46ff where Bartimaeus persisted in crying out to Jesus. In James 5:15 we see that prayers of intercession for others are valid as well as James writes about the *"prayer offered in faith."* In Mark chapter 5, Jairus comes seeking healing on behalf of his little daughter.

Prayers from God are more direct; they often take the form of a command for healing to come and can be God initiated and given. This is the primary form of healing ministry that Jesus used. He told the man with the withered hand in Mark 3:1-5 to *"stretch out your hand"* (v. 5). Commands require faith for the healing to manifest, and this kind of faith is God's faith given for a specific situation. I have discussed this in chapter 2.

4. Prayer Engagement: The ministry team is now ready to begin ministering using the previously selected prayers. Several helpful hints while ministering will be offered here. First, keep your eyes open while praying so you can observe what is happening. When we first started ministering healing, I was quite religious and would close my eyes while praying. I once was praying enthusiastically for a woman with my hand outstretched over her head. When I finished praying and opened my eyes, I found the woman stretched out on the floor as she had been overcome by the power of the Spirit. I heard of a pastor who did the same one time after a service, but when he opened his eyes the woman was gone. Her husband had gotten tired of waiting for the pastor to finish praying and had taken his wife home!

We also believe it is important to stay calm and minister without hype. We need to let God be God and not try to make something happen by our own actions. We can't heal anyone on our own anyway. This doesn't mean that the prayer can't be spoken firmly; it just means that we don't want to solicit a response that is not authentic.

Ask the Holy Spirit for help while you minister, and keep your attention focused on the person receiving ministry. Don't let your eyes and mind wander while praying. If you do get distracted, don't get too upset; God can use you anyway. I once observed a young man on John Wimber's team from California ministering to a young woman who was ill in one of our meetings. He was quite young, possibly in his late teens, and was dressed very casually in shorts, T-shirt, and without shoes. As he prayed over Cheryl, "Come Holy Spirit," he was looking around and chewing gum. I remember thinking, *Lord, couldn't you have brought someone else to pray for Cheryl, she's really sick and needs to be healed.* Well, even though he didn't seem to be focused on Cheryl, the Lord was. Cheryl began to shake under the power of the Spirit and she was totally healed.

Look for effects while you are ministering. Sometimes your hand will become warm or the person receiving ministry will say your hand is hot even though you don't feel anything. Other common effects are the body shaking, eyelids fluttering, tears, deep sighs, the skin becoming flushed, or the sensing of the presence of the Lord. Manifestations of the Spirit are not necessary for healing to come, but they encourage us while we minister that something is happening.

Don't be in a hurry. You can pause and see how the person receiving ministry is feeling or if they discern anything happening during prayer. Many times when we pray with someone who has pain in their body, they can report that the pain is lessening and this prompts us to continue to minister to see if the pain can diminish even more.

Above all, stay open to the leading of the Holy Spirit. He may have you stop for a bit or He may show you the need to go in a different direction. Once when I was ministering to a woman in Hamburg, Germany, the pain she had kept jumping from place to place in her body. As I prayed over one area, the pain would leave but then it would reappear in a different part of her body. I was perplexed and called another team member over to help. He was more prophetic than I and immediately discerned that we were dealing with a spirit of pain that was moving around on her. We took authority over this spirit, commanded it to leave, spoke healing to the woman, and everything was fine.

5. Post Prayer Direction: Although we are not professional counselors, some post prayer advice may be appropriate. People receiving ministry may need encouragement to pursue the normal Christian disciplines of Bible study, prayer, staying in fellowship, etc. Depending upon the individual situation, they may need to seek follow-up counseling from a pastor or other professional in order to sustain or complete the healing process. We also advise those on medications to not change them without confirmation from their physician. However, they also need to be alert to adverse side effects from the medications as healing occurs. For example, I ministered to a diabetic in California during a training school and the Lord touched her in a significant way. As she administered her insulin the next day, she began to have a reaction and needed to consume orange juice and some candy to reverse the reaction. It took her a couple of days to get her blood sugar stabilized and she consulted her doctor on returning home.

Healing Rooms

Since 1999 healing rooms have blossomed in many cities and nations. Doris and I are connected with the International Association of Healing Rooms headquartered in Spokane, Washington, under the direction of Cal Pierce and his team. We have operated healing rooms in the Kansas City area since 2002, with many positive healings to report. Actually, we ministered to people in settings similar to what we now do in the healing rooms before 1999, but we didn't call those sessions by this name. We would simply have ministry teams available at certain locations at specific times and we would minister to the sick or hurting that came for prayer. We have also been blessed to be part of bringing the healing room concept to other nations.

Basically, the healing room provides a setting where the information we have discussed so far can be applied to the sick. A location is established with regular published hours when the rooms will be available to the public. The setting is similar to a doctor's office where a receptionist will greet the person coming for prayer, give them a short form to fill out, and ask them to wait for the next available ministry team. The form provides some background information for the team along with the specific healing request. Ministry teams are trained to pray and bring healing to those that come to the healing rooms. Normally a team of two or three will minister to an individual for from ten to twenty minutes. It is not a counseling ministry but an opportunity to receive healing for a physical issue. Some deliverance may be necessary to achieve healing, but these sessions are not designed to be a time when extensive deliverance is ministered. If major deliverance is deemed necessary, a separate appointment is made with a team experienced in this sort of ministry.

Those who minister in healing rooms, or anywhere for that matter, need to have an attitude of compassion for the sick, rejected, and hurting. Often someone who comes to the healing room for healing may lack knowledge and experience with God's healing love. They may be desperately ill and have been referred to the healing rooms by a friend as a last-ditch effort to get well. They may be completely without faith in God's healing power but are hoping that something good can happen. In these situations, the team must be aware of where the requester is in their faith walk and help them build up their faith with scripture and testimonies of those that have been healed, especially from the condition they are now experiencing.

People who have been sick for a long time often have given up hope of being healed. They may have been prayed for several times, and possibly from some traveling ministers noted for seeing multiple healings in their meetings without any positive results. They may have suffered disappointment, depression or despair, and are weary of life itself. The prayer minister must take the time to encourage them that Jesus is still the healer, that their miracle of healing may be just one prayer away. We must be careful not to judge where the sick person is in their faith; the entire Christian church has been taught doubt and unbelief for centuries. We can sympathize with the sick individual but our job is to encourage them and lead them to the truth.

Detailed information regarding locating a healing room near the reader can be obtained from the International Association of Healing Rooms, 112 East First Ave., Spokane, WA, 99202, or from their website: www.healingrooms.com. They also provide information and help for those desiring to start a healing room in their area. When Cal Pierce is asked if someone should start a healing room in their community, he often replies, "Do you have any sick there?"

I'll share just a few of the many, many healing testimonies we have recorded from our healing rooms:

Teresa: Came with *shoulder, arm and neck pain*. Could not turn neck. Pain is gone and neck turns without pain.

Rick: PTL! My *neck and back pain* from car wreck lingered even after treatment. The prayer team laid hands on me and immediately I felt the strong presence of the Lord. As they prayed, all my muscles, ligaments, and soft tissue loosened up and I had *pain-free mobility*. Praise Jesus!

Sharon: I'm now *drug free*. Even the desire for drugs is gone. I've been free for about three months now. I'm in church and school. *(Note: Sharon is still free over a year later.)*

Fay: Fay came with *stomach pain* which she said she had for three weeks. She left without pain after prayer.

Romika: She was *paralyzed* on the left side, *hand and arm*, from a car accident twenty-five years ago. After prayer, she could move both her hand and arm.

Patrick: I was diagnosed with *diabetes* in 2009. I got prayer several times, and no longer need to take diabetes medicine. My blood sugar level has dropped through prayer. Thank You, Jesus!

Jesse: I *hurt my arm* while working. I could not bend it all the way. After prayer, it was 99+ percent better. No pain and it has flexibility.

Kim: I went to the eye doc this week and *my eye* is doing fantastic! Vision improved to 20/30 for months now! What's even more amazing is God's grace and healing! Had new pictures taken and the scar in my central vision is even more prominent and by all accounts, should not be able to see at all let alone 20/30!!! Praise Him! All day long!!! *(Note: This is an on-going, continuous miracle. Medically speaking, Kim cannot see; but she does!)*

Ramona: I came asking for prayer for healing for these areas: *kidneys, pancreas, myopathy, stroke, and seizures.* You prayed for me several times, including the Children's Healing Ministry, and now I have 95 percent healing in my three fingers, 95 percent healing in my shoulder, and my mind is restored to 95 percent cognitive ability. *(This is an abbreviated testimony; Ramona gave us a detailed testimony that runs for a page and a half. The Lord also settled Ramona's $500,000 medical expenses.)*

CHAPTER 6

Healing in the Glory

In recent years, several prophetic ministers have been speaking and teaching about the *glory*. They often explain that God is doing something new; speak about the glory realm; and then have miracles, signs, healings, and wonders happen during their meetings. Signs and wonders such as feathers or jewels appearing apparently out of the atmosphere, spontaneous healings within the assembled crowd, gold fillings or crowns materializing in someone's mouth, and other wonderful events cause us all to marvel at our awesome, loving God. Often when the minister senses the presence of the Lord in the room, he or she will rapidly call out several words of knowledge and encourage people to check their bodies to see if any change has occurred. Traveling ministers such as Patricia King and David Herzog teach on the glory realm at conferences and seminars around the world. Their books on this subject are available in Christian bookstores and online.

Exactly what is meant by the "glory"? This term as used in the preceding paragraph applies only to the glory of God. Paul tells us that there are different kinds of glory; there is a glory of a heavenly body, glory of an earthly body, a glory of the sun, etc. (1 Corinthians 15:40-41). Glory, when used in the context discussed here, refers only to the glory of God. As I understand it, God's glory is closely associated with the activity of the Holy Spirit and can be thought of as the weighty, manifest presence of God. I like to call it the "unveiled presence of God," referring back to the veil that covered the face of Moses as the skin of his face shone from being in the presence of God; and then remembering that the veil in the temple was torn in two as Jesus died on the cross, thus ensuring that we can enter boldly into His presence (Hebrews 4:16). Paul had this in mind when he wrote: *"But we all, with unveiled face, beholding as in a mirror the glory of the Lord…just as from the Lord, the Spirit"* (2 Corinthians 3:18). According to the footnote for Exodus 26:33 in Ryrie's NASB, a first century historian, Josephus, writes that this veil that separated the Holy of Holies, where God's presence dwelt, from the Holy Place was four inches thick and was so strong that horses could not tear it apart. Now, under the new covenant, we believers can go through the torn veil and experience God's presence, His glory.

I'm not convinced that seeing God act in this way is a "new discovery," but perhaps it is a "rediscovery" of God's goodness being poured out in this manner. Ministers from a previous era such as Kathryn Kuhlman and William Branham were noted for calling out accurate words of knowledge followed by people coming forward to confirm that a healing had happened. The words of knowledge were frequently given after an extended time of worship and praise. We see something similar today in the ministries of Benny Hinn, Bill Johnson, and Randy Clark. What seems to be happening is that God is once again awakening the Body to minister and receive healing in this manner. If the Holy Spirit is emphasizing this type of ministry today; He has a reason for it, and we all need to be sensitive to the Spirit and cooperate whether the methodology is familiar to us or not.

I attended my second Glory Invasion Conference in the fall of 2013. Speakers at this conference were Kevin Basconi and David and Stephanie Herzog. They taught specifically on the glory with many wonderful results being reported. Many people had dental miracles of one kind or another; several received gold crowns or fillings. One woman who received a cold crown or filling at the beginning of the conference had it turn to porcelain by the end of the meetings. Another man who had several fillings from prior dental work found that all his fillings had turned to tooth. He no longer had the evidence of previous dental work. Many backs and necks that had pain or restricted motion were healed, as well as the face of a man who had half of his face paralyzed. Some tumors and cysts disappeared, a

Lutheran pastor had his hearing restored, and a young woman who needed a cane to walk now no longer needed the cane. Perhaps some of the most amazing wonders occurred as a few experienced supernatural weight loss; they needed to hold up their pants as their girth was no longer sufficient to hold up their garments. All of the healings and wonders mentioned here occurred in the glory of God and without the laying on of hands; it was from the presence of God, His glory. Yet, some who desperately needed healing from such serious illnesses such as cancer and multiple sclerosis were not touched in any significant way. Why, you say? Why wasn't the one with cancer or MS healed? Why give gold crowns or feathers and not touch the critically ill? This leaves us to wonder, doesn't it? God is still God, and He alone knows the answers to questions such as these. We rejoice in what we see and continue to ask for what needs yet to be done.

The Glory Invasion Conference mentioned above consisted of ten sessions from Thursday evening until Monday, and two of those days had only one session. Thus, with three meetings in a day, my commitment to work in the conference bookstore before and after sessions, and driving to and from the meeting place for a half hour each way, I was quite tired near the end of the conference. Arriving home on Sunday evening about 11 p.m., I played a message left on our answering machine. It was a request for me to speak at the next evening's meeting at Hope City, a downtown ministry of which we are a part. My first response was no, I'm too tired to put something together for tomorrow. But I realized that asking me to speak on such short notice was probably an indication that they were having some trouble getting a speaker for the meeting. Perhaps the speaker they had scheduled had to cancel for some reason. So reluctantly I agreed to speak, thinking that I could probably put a teaching together from some notes of previous messages I had given elsewhere.

The following morning (Monday) as I sought the Lord on what to speak on that evening, He made it very clear that I was to speak on what I had been exposed to during the conference, i.e., the glory realm. I argued with Him, as I had not read the books yet (have you ever argued with God? If so, who won?). I had purchased several of the speakers' books at the conference but they not yet been opened. God won, and I found myself presenting information and testimonies from the conference Monday evening at Hope City. At the close of my teaching, I asked if they were willing to see if God would come with His presence, His glory. The group was enthusiastic about seeking God in this manner. So, after an additional time of praise and worship and upon sensing the Spirit's presence, I led them in an enthusiastic shout of praise and acclamation to the Lord. Immediately I received and called out several words of knowledge. As I remember now, someone responded to almost every word of knowledge and testified to their healing. Also, the atmosphere remained charged with the presence of God and the leader of the meeting asked those still needing healing to identify themselves. Then, teams of two or three nearby people laid hands on those needing healing and several more testimonies of healings were given. It was a wonderful experience.

Some Thoughts on the Glory Realm

Since that Hope City meeting, I have spent considerable time researching God's glory from the scriptures. I have some additional thoughts on the glory that I would like to share with you here.

> We were created to know and experience God's glory, His unveiled presence (Isaiah 43:7; John 17:22, 24; Romans 9:23). In fact, we are instructed to seek the glory that comes from God (John 5:44; 7:18).
>
> Healing and our sharing testimonies of God's goodness in healing the sick bring glory to God (John 11:4; Luke 5:25-26; Luke 7:16).
>
> The whole earth will one day be filled with the glory of God (Numbers 14:21; Isaiah 6:3; Habakkuk 2:14).

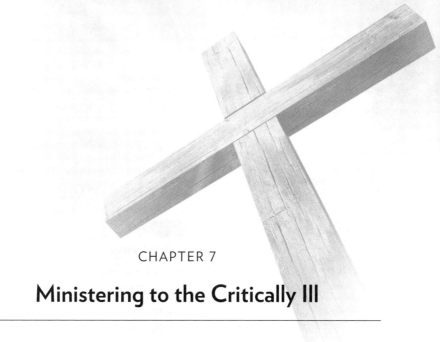

CHAPTER 7

Ministering to the Critically Ill

Those of us who minister healing to others and have seen the Lord move powerfully on so many occasions long for the time when everyone we pray for is healed by the power of God. Often we come into desperate, life-threatening situations and we go away sad and frustrated when the healing does not come. Why do we see so many backs and limbs healed when those stricken with cancer or aids are seldom healed? Jesus proclaimed the gospel and healed every kind of sickness and disease (Matthew 4:23-24). He hasn't changed. He still is willing to heal every kind of sickness or disease. Do we need more power, more anointing? Must we be more holy for God to pour out His Spirit upon us? Do we lack spiritual maturity? Haven't we all asked ourselves these questions? Certainly I have. We are not walking in the power of God that we should be. We need more anointing. We should be more holy than we are because God Himself lives within us.

Yet, it is all by grace, His grace. As with the apostle Paul, we are given grace from God to minister to others (Ephesians 3:2). I can do nothing on my own, just as Jesus did nothing on His own but only what He saw the Father doing. He alone is my adequacy (2 Corinthians 3:5). I cannot make myself more holy or infuse more power into my prayers by some word or deed on my part. I must learn how to cooperate more fully with the Holy Spirit. He is my Leader, my Source, my Guide in these difficult situations. While before the Crucifixion Jesus taught and instructed the disciples, now

He gives His instructions through the person of the Holy Spirit. So we ask Holy Spirit, what are we to do here and now with this one who is so critically ill?

When someone dear to us becomes very ill, haven't we wished that they could be prayed for by one of those who have demonstrated great healing powers? Someone like Charles or Frances Hunter, or Francis MacNutt, or Oral Roberts, or Kathryn Kuhlman, or Mahesh Chavda, or John Wimber, or, perhaps, Jesus Himself. But, Jesus said that it was to our advantage that He go away because He would send us the Holy Spirit (John 16:7). I believe He wants us all to learn how to depend on our Helper, the Holy Spirit, to do these healing works which in turn will glorify His name.

I've struggled with these issues for thirty-five years. I've learned a few things. Perhaps if you can glean from what we have learned and add that to what you have learned, even more critically ill people can be made well again. I do believe that a primary reason we do not see more people healed is the lack of unity within the body of Christ. Many sincere Christians believe that God does not want to heal everyone; He may heal some now and then but certainly He would not want all to be healed. They have not been taught correctly.

We have two basic models that seem to show promise when praying for the critically ill. They are described below. By and large, the people that these models are directed toward will have given up hope for any fullness of life except the Lord intervene on their behalf. These models do not represent the final answer on how to heal the sick, but they do provide other vehicles for the Lord to use in ministering His love and healing power in critical situations. We have had some notable success ministering in this fashion, but still, we have more to learn. Following these guidelines has enabled us to see some marvelous healings, but we have also been disappointed in situations where the healing did not manifest. God never intended us to have to wait until someone with an international healing ministry comes to town for healings to occur in our community. These models are a starting point for anyone who chooses to minister to the critically ill.

Model 1: Group Intercession for an Individual Who Is Not Present

In this model, a group of people, say ten to twenty individuals, gather together to intercede for one particular person or problem. The critically ill person is not present; perhaps they are bed ridden or in an intensive care unit in a hospital. I will focus my remarks here on group intercession for the healing of someone who is critically ill, although this same model can be used effectively for other issues. Before I describe how a typical group session might unfold, let me first discuss a couple of key points.

Importance of Unity

It is very important that everyone that gathers to intercede for the sick individual be in basic agreement that they believe God heals and that His will is healing for the person that is ill. God promises that His mature church will be in unity (Ephesians 4:13) and that God Himself will command the blessing when we live together in unity (Psalm 133). Unity is so powerful when ministering to the sick. In the 14th chapter of John, verse 14, Jesus declares: *"If you ask Me anything in My name, I will do it."* In our modern day translations, we lose sight of the significance of the "you" in this passage. It is a collective you, "ye" in the old King James Version, not a singular you, "thee." In other words, Jesus is saying to the church at large that *if we together ask Him, He will do it.*

We first noticed this blessing from unity when we were ministering in our community-wide prayer group in Rapid City. We saw many interesting healings take place when that group prayed for someone and we were convinced that the Lord was giving us special grace because the group was comprised of Lutherans, Baptists, Pentecostals, etc. Denominational walls had been set aside as the group came together on a weekly basis to worship Him, share our lives with each other, and pray for the sick.

The power in unified prayer is tremendous. An example of this power is a time that Doris and I felt lead to call the Christians of the Rapid City community together for a day of prayer and fasting to oppose the moral degradation that was occurring. We arranged for a large meeting area and advertised the event in the Rapid City Daily Journal, the local newspaper. The Lord gave us the wisdom to split the area for prayer into two primary sections, one for those who wished to pray aloud and one for those who wished to pray silently. In this way, we thought that those who wished to pray in tongues would not offend those who did not believe in praying in tongues as they were more likely to want to pray silently instead of out loud. The Lord was ahead of us there as well. I remember how blessed I was to witness the pastor of the Evangelical Free Church seat himself in the midst of some charismatics who were praying in tongues.

We had good participation at our little event and the Lord gave us results beyond our greatest expectations. Within a few days after the day of prayer and fasting, we began to see things happen. Within a few weeks:

> An escort service which doubled as a prostitution ring was broken up by police.

> The only X-rated theater in Rapid City was closed for repairs. It remained closed for over a decade after the prayer meeting, and was later demolished and another business was constructed in its location.

> A local gang-operated nightclub, which was notorious for its risqué activities, was the scene of a shooting and was closed for investigation. The investigation eventually split the gang, closed the club, and the building is now used for another business.

We should not be surprised by the power available to a group of unified, committed Christians. The Tower of Babel (Genesis 11:6) is an indicator of this unified power as is our Lord's announcement that He and the Father were unified (John 10:30). We see this principle of unity operating in the early church as those who believed with *one* heart and soul were given great power and abundant grace (Acts 4:32-33).

The effects of disunity within the church can also be documented. Over the centuries, healings done within the church seem to have gone from:

All in the early church (Acts 5:16) to *Many* (Acts 8:7) to *Some* or possibly *Few* in the current church.

Between Acts 5 and Acts 8 we witness the first major quarrel within the early church regarding the distribution of daily resources (Acts 6:1ff).

By AD 55 quarrels and strife within the body caused Paul to address the problem (1 Corinthians 10ff).

Protection by Group Intercession

James 4:6 says, *"God is opposed to the proud, but gives grace to the humble."* Any act of God is by grace, and healing is no exception. We need His grace to minister in this difficult area; but when a major healing does come, we have the human tendency to be proud that God used us as a healing channel. Then if we become proud healers, the Lord is resolved to oppose us until we are humbled once more. Ministering in a large group avoids the pitfall of thinking we are somebody special because God used us.

When several people are praying for the Lord to heal the same ill person, one is lead to pray this way while another will pray something different. Sometimes all pray in tongues together. If positive results are reported after the intercessory session is completed regarding the one who is ill, no one who participated in the group prayer would be foolish enough to think that it was his or her prayer alone that caused the healing or improvement. For the Christian there is some truth in the old saying, "there is safety in numbers."

Biblical Example

A good example of group intercession is found in Acts 12:5-17. In this story, the church was fervently requesting God to deliver Peter from prison. God answered by sending an angel to free him even though Peter was chained to two soldiers. The church was still gathered for prayer when Peter showed up at Mark's house. Although this biblical example does not discuss a group meeting together for the purpose of petitioning God for someone's healing, it seems safe to assume that they would use this mode for healing as well as for other difficult circumstances.

Suggested Format

Although we always try to listen for the Lord's direction, we generally follow the format that the early church used in Acts 4:24. Here we find a group of believers gathered and together they lift *"their voices to God with one accord."* From this we can deduce that, as we have already indicated, unity of purpose is important; and in addition they all seem to pray and possibly all prayed at the same time. Steve Bostrum, a Mexican missionary who visited us, said that at their prayer meetings they all prayed out loud, and very loud, at the same time. I frequently tell those who gather at these prayer sessions that it is only in America that we think God can only listen to one of us at a time.

A typical intercessory session might proceed like this:

Someone we know is critically ill. It may be cancer or some other terminal illness or it may be a situation where medicine does not seem to have any answers such as blindness.

We issue an announcement for prayer giving the meeting location and time. If the person is known within the congregation, we would probably make the announcement at a church service. If the individual is not known at our church, then we would make an effort to contact his or her circle of believing friends and invite them for a time of prayer.

Once we gather at the appointed place, a leader gives just a few instructions and opens the meeting with prayer. The primary instructions are:

1. Everyone is welcome to pray and to pray in tongues as well. This is an invited, believer's meeting and praying in tongues will not violate Paul's admonition in 1 Corinthians 14:23.

2. All can pray quietly to God either in tongues or English at the same time.

3. As the Holy Spirit quickens a certain way to pray to someone, they should raise their voice to be heard above the others. When this occurs, others praying should reduce their volume so the first individual can be heard. After the direction of the prayer is heard, the other individuals should agree in prayer using this direction for such time as the Holy Spirit seems to indicate. For example, as we are praying, someone may feel strongly that they should pray for the immune system to

function properly. Others would chime in with similar prayers such as God declaring that the life of the flesh is in the blood (Leviticus 17:11) and the immune system carried by the blood must begin to function again, etc. This would continue until the Spirit allows the prayers to once more fall down to background level and then another person might be quicken to lead out in prayer in a different direction.

4. Prayer should continue until there is general agreement that the Holy Spirit has released the group. This might be thirty minutes, an hour, or more. If someone needs to leave for some reason, they should feel free to do so.

Personal Experiences

We do not routinely schedule these kinds of sessions for everyone that we know is ill. There seems to be a need for a certain level of Spirit-directed interest and energy before we can muster the incentive to organize a group prayer time and have people respond to the invitation. We have been privileged to witness a couple of miraculous healings where someone was given up for dead and now has been brought back to wonderful health. We believe that the group intercessory prayer times that we had for these individuals were vital keys to their recovery.

Our first experience in using this type of group intercession for healing was when our dear friend Sharon contacted leukemia. Sharon was a forty-four year old, single female, who lived alone. She had adult children and was a long time, faithful member of Kansas City Fellowship (now renamed Metro Christian Fellowship). In December of 1989 she was diagnosed with an aggressive type of leukemia which soon had her undergoing massive doses of chemotherapy. Several complications arose during treatment and Sharon was left with some problems from the treatment including a damaged heart.

Sharon had received a word from the Lord regarding life, not death, before she learned of her illness. She recorded in her prayer journal that she "would live and not die." We clung to this promise from the Lord as we prayed for her.

Many people from the congregation loved Sharon deeply so it seemed natural for us to come together to pray for her. We gathered for group prayer as her life hung in the balance. I am certain that we met more than once, but I don't remember whether it was two or three different times. Sharon underwent treatment in January and February of 1990 and was discharged with her leukemia in remission on March 9, 1990. Her damaged heart was completely healed which remains beyond medical logic.

Upon discharge, Sharon was told that should the leukemia ever reoccur that she could not be treated for it. The massive chemical doses which her body had been given and the damage she retained, especially to her heart, would preclude her receiving treatment again as the chemical treatment itself would kill her. In 1995, Sharon was once again diagnosed with leukemia. The healing she received from her first bout with this disease allowed for her medical treatment again. She responded to treatment remarkably well and her leukemia was once again in remission.

Another successful experience with group intercessory prayer for healing came in 1992. A woman from our congregation made some missionary trips to Nigeria. During one of her trips, she apparently was bitten by a mosquito and contacted a potentially fatal form of malaria. This was unknown to Shirley when she began her initial visits to her physician in July.

Shirley lived in Harrisonville, a small community located about twenty miles south of Kansas City. It is not surprising that a family doctor in a small community in Missouri did not immediately recognize the symptoms of malaria. Shirley was first hospitalized in Harrisonville on the first of August. She fell into a coma and was transferred to Research Hospital in Kansas City on August fifth. At this time Shirley was in a coma and on life support systems. Her blood pressure hovered near 65, her kidneys were failing, there was little oxygen transfer through her blood, she was on dialysis, was jaundiced, and had a lung infection. Her children had been called and told that Shirley was dying as she was not responding to the medication to bring her blood pressure up. Shirley believes that it was the prayers of the saints that brought her blood pressure up enough that dialysis could be administered.

During this time when she was near death, Shirley had a vision of a little girl holding the Lord's hand. She was stumbling and was tired; her head only came about up to His knee as He was tall. She knew that the little girl was her and she said, "Father, I'm so tired, please help me." She asked Him to make her whole again. She remembers that the Lord picked her up and carried her like a small child.

Shirley was placed in an Intensive Care Unit and was diagnosed with malaria by the medical staff at Research. Her physician later gave a presentation to the medical staff on Shirley's illness where he stated that her type of malaria was known to be potentially fatal, and the U.S. generally saw three to five deaths annually from this disease. He further stated that if more than 5 percent of the red blood cells in a patient's system were affected that the situation was considered life threatening. It was impossible to determine exactly the percentage of red blood cells affected in Shirley's system, but he was sure that it was more than 90 percent. Even if Shirley were to recover, the lack of oxygen to her organs and the build up of toxins in her blood were projected to cause major consequences. Major organs of concern were the brain, heart, lungs, liver, and kidneys.

A team of pastors from the church prayed for Shirley while she was unconscious in ICU and Shirley's friends and relative prayed for her as well. On August 16, sixteen days after Shirley was initially hospitalized, we held an organized group intercessory prayer time for Shirley's healing. On August 24 Shirley was discharged from ICU. By September 10, sufficient tests had been completed to indicate that Shirley's heart, brain, liver and lungs were okay. Her kidneys were estimated to be functioning at 90 percent but were improving.

At different times Shirley would become alert and would remind herself that she must continue to praise the Lord and remember that nothing was too difficult for God and that all His promises were true. She now believes that these periods of alertness would come just after someone had prayed for her or read scripture. She cautions those of us who minister to the critically ill that our spirit never sleeps and that we should be careful to speak positive things when in the sickroom.

Shirley continues in good health. She has become quite active in a local congregation in Harrisonville so she no longer regularly makes the trip to worship with us in Kansas City. Some of the staff at Research Hospital were aware that we were laying hands on Shirley and praying for her healing while she was in ICU. They have been known to say, "That lady must live right," which is their response to Shirley's recovery. We know who the Healer was. We are truly grateful for the Lord's intervention to bring about this healing.

Model II: Team Prayer with an Individual Who Is Present
We have occasionally gathered small teams of four to six people to pray for someone who was ill. At least from our perspective, we have had mixed results from this approach in that success in healing very critical illnesses sometimes has eluded us; but much personal ministry normally occurs at these sessions. Generally both the individual and the ministry team are encouraged and uplifted during these sessions.

A typical situation for which we would assemble a prayer team would be for someone with a long-term, chronic illness such as multiple sclerosis or diabetes. We believe that a small team like this is the perfect setting for assembling individuals with different gifts that could possibly hold a key for healing the one who is ill. Christians with prophetic ministries should be present in addition to those who have been used in healing.

As I mentioned above, there is protection in praying as a group or team. No matter how sincere we are about giving God *all* the glory, our flesh tends to become a little puffed up when He uses us.

Biblical Examples

There are several scriptural examples of a small group or team of people gathering for prayer. In Acts 1:12-14 we see that the eleven apostles, at least three women (Luke 8:2-3), the Lord's mother, and His four brothers were praying together. We cannot be certain that their prayers included prayer for those needing healing, but it seems likely in view of the prayer recorded in Acts 4:23ff where they requested the Lord to heal as well as perform other signs and wonders.

In James 5:14, one who is sick is specifically told to call for the elders (a prayer team) to come and pray over him. This scripture gives us some guidance regarding the make-up of our prayer team. Elders would not be new converts, they would have a mature faith, they would have experienced God's interaction in their own lives, and they would be expected to be receptive to being used by the Holy Spirit in the exercising of spiritual gifts.

Format

The atmosphere for ministry should be designed to put the team and the one being ministered to at ease. Someone's living room would be a normal setting provided the home is generally quiet and interruptions can be avoided. A ministry team should consist of at least 3 and no more than 6 individuals. Larger groups than four or five tend to be intimidating for sharing especially when the sharing approaches events of a personal nature.

A short time of worship or the reading of scripture are excellent ways to wash everyone's mind from their own busy day and circumstances which allows the Holy Spirit to have His way a little easier. Generally by the time worship is over, someone from the team will have received some revelation from the Lord which should be taken as the beginning point for ministry. Revelation should always be given with grace in a manner that allows the person to decline that the revelation is true without feeling condemned or judged by those present. This should be followed even if rejecting the revelation blocks the healing process. The individual is already ill; they need to be treated with respect. It may be that after thinking about some revelation for a time, that a change of heart will occur which will allow God to do a much deeper work than is possible at the time of the current session.

Prayer would proceed along the lines of what revelation is given, but it is not limited to just new spiritual information. As the session progresses, all the team members should be given an opportunity to pray and minister as they feel led. A typical session will normally run for an hour or two; so if that time frame is understood before the group assembles, it avoids operating under pressure to complete the session to meet someone's particular schedule.

Personal Experiences

The first major healing that Doris and I were part of came in a small team setting as described above. I have already described the healing of Mary's back in chapter 4 on physical healing as a small group of us gathered at her bedside to pray for healing. On other occasions it seemed as if we gathered to pray for physical healing but the Lord had other things on His agenda.

One such time was when a small group of us assembled to pray for Sue, a young woman in our congregation with a serious eye ailment. Sue

HEALING AND DELIVERANCE FUNDAMENTALS

had been diagnosed as a teenager with eye problems and was told that she would probably be blind by the time she was twenty. Sue was slightly beyond twenty years of age when the team ministered to her, and she was not blind but her vision was severely restricted. In laymen's terms we would call it "tunnel vision" in that she could only see directly ahead of her and did not have any peripheral vision.

Sue and her mother came for prayer and we began with a short time of worship. As worship was concluded, one of the team members asked Sue about fear. He said that the Lord had said, "Freedom from fear." Immediately, Sue broke into tears and through her sobs shared that she was gripped by fear; it was a major factor in her life. Her reduced vision caused her to be fearful as she was sometimes startled by someone or something being near her but unseen because of her lack of peripheral vision. She shared that when she came home in the evening after work that she would carefully check out each room in the apartment to be absolutely sure that no unwanted visitor was present. Her fear was strong enough to keep her from showering unless her husband was present in the house. The Lord graciously delivered Sue from her fear and then we proceeded to pray for the healing of her eyes. Sue shared a few days later that she had been set free from the oppressive fear she had labored with for many years; but to our knowledge, there has not been any improvement in her eyesight.

We have used this small group format for others and the Lord has always helped us minister. A young woman I will call Aby was ministered to by our small group one evening. Aby was a veterinarian that was experiencing major physical reactions to a variety of chemicals and other environmental factors. This was a serious problem for her as she handled many different chemicals as part of her vocation. She had pursued medical remedies and was to the point of trying to sell her house and move into a specially constructed environmentally clean home after spending time in a detoxification center in Texas. As you might imagine, these kinds of solutions were disruptive to her life as well as being very expensive.

When we prayed for Aby, one of the team members had a vision of her being in a swing as a little girl. Aby knew exactly what this was about as it related to an event from her childhood. One day in an attempt to gain some attention, Aby pretended to get hurt by falling out of her swing.

Additional wisdom came forth and Aby received ministry and inner healing for some personal aspects of her life. She is better now, but not as a result of our prayers for physical healing. She went ahead with the medical treatment and spent several weeks in the detoxification center in an environmentally clean environment.

In summary then, I would say that our experiences with ministering to an individual with a small prayer team have been positive but incomplete. We have always felt the Lord's presence and approval about what happened during the ministry session, and I believe that every single person we have ministered to in this setting has been appreciative and blessed by the process. This alone should be enough encouragement for us to continue with this type of ministry. Yet, this method, as well as others, is not a formula we can use so everyone is healed.

CHAPTER 8

What to Do when Healing Doesn't Come

Unfortunately we do not always see positive results when we minister to the sick. This chapter deals with the very real question of what to do when we have labored in prayer for someone's healing and it does not manifest. Here are some dos and don'ts.

Do Not Quit: Satan wants you to quit. If he can get a soldier or leader to put down his battle weapons, then he has won that fight. He won't have to worry about you again. If those of us who understand that it is God's will to heal do not contend for healing, who will? Certainly unbelievers and nominal Christians will not carry on this fight. It is a fight. We don't always win, but as Doris says, "Quitting is not an option."

Several years ago when we were in the midst of fighting for a healing for a critically ill person, we were tempted to give up the fight. We were not seeing the progress we so desired. As Doris was meditating on the resurrection of Lazarus in John 11, she clearly heard the voice of the Lord: "Just because I haven't come yet does not mean that you are to decide that I'm not coming at all." It was a not so gentle rebuke that we have taken to heart in these situations.

Perhaps the healing we seek is just a prayer, a day, or a week away. If we quit, we will not receive that which we desire. While we don't always know the outcome if we do pray; we do know the outcome if we *don't* pray. When we don't pray, we never obtain the miracle we seek.

Jesus Himself told us not to quit. In Luke 11:9-10 He told us to ask and keep asking, seek and keep seeking, knock and keep knocking. Again, quitting is not an option.

Do Not Be Discouraged: I get discouraged too easily. It is something I must be aware of and fight off. Perhaps you do too. When we don't see happen what we expect and want to see, it seems too hard to go on and fight again. Remember nobody sees everybody they pray for healed; you are not alone. Even the prophet Elijah became discouraged when he heard that Jezebel was looking for him; and this was just after a major victory over the prophets of Baal on Mt. Carmel (1 Kings 18). Randy Clark has a two CD set that has helped me shake discouragement; it is titled *The Thrill of Victory and the Agony of Defeat*. It is available on the Global Awakening website.

Make an effort to stay encouraged in the Lord. Keep your focus on what you see God doing in your life and the lives of those around you. Share testimonies with each other; they are so important. Read and meditate on the Word of God. Paul tells us that the Word was written so God could give us perseverance and encouragement so we could continue in hope (Romans 15:4-5). Without hope that people will be healed when we minister to them, we will not be effective.

Do Not Blame Yourself: There is always the tendency to look within ourselves when healing doesn't happen. We know the problem does not lie with God so it is normal to wonder if it is because we have not done something or we have done something incorrectly. In some cases this may actually be true, but if it is, rely on the Holy Spirit to let you know and to correct you. Navel gazing is not productive. By our own efforts we cannot heal anyone. We cannot make ourselves more holy, more anointed, more righteous. Jesus is the healer and we are only the channels of His love.

Although Paul points to his ministry being founded in the demonstration of the Spirit and the power of God (1 Corinthians 2:4), he clearly understood that the source of the demonstrations of power were not from within him. He states that our adequacy is from God and He has made us ministers of the new covenant through the Holy Spirit (2 Corinthians 3:5-6).

Do Not Blame the Person Receiving Ministry: Healing ministers have been known to tell someone, "If you only had more faith, you would be healed." What a terrible burden to place on someone. We have seen unbelievers, those completely without faith in God or His healing power, healed so if there is a lack of faith somewhere it may be in the one ministering healing, not the person receiving ministry. Don't add another burden to the one already struggling with sickness or disease.

That being said, sometimes the one receiving ministry has a stumbling block that the Lord wants to remove before He completes the healing process. However, if the Lord is dealing with a person it is better to let Him point out the stumbling block rather than the healing minister. An interesting situation we encountered one time was when we were attending a Sunday evening service at the local Episcopalian church. I received a word of knowledge regarding the healing of hemorrhoids. I was somewhat hesitant to give this word publically, especially in the setting we were in. I knew the priest personally, so decided to just give him a note about the hemorrhoids and suggest that the individual with this problem ask the Lord to heal them as we took communion that evening. He wasn't any more anxious then I was to have the individual publically identify themselves as having hemorrhoids so he did as I suggested and we all just went home after the service. The following Friday, at the local Women's Aglow meeting, a lady identified herself as the individual with the hemorrhoids. She had been at the Episcopalian service, had done as the priest and I had suggested, but had not been healed. I offered to pray for her once again and as I did so she began to fall out under the power of the Holy Spirit but quickly grabbed my arm to steady herself and keep from falling. About a week later, I received a call from the lady's husband explaining that she still had not been healed but they thought they knew why. They asked to come over for prayer once again, which I agreed to do. When they arrived, the lady explained that she felt pride was an issue. She was the president of the local Women's Aglow chapter and did not think it was fitting for her to fall out under the power of the Holy Spirit; hence, this is why she grabbed my arm when I prayed for her. She asked to stand while I prayed for her again, and she repented before the Lord of her pride and of wanting her healing to be done her way. She fell under the power of the Spirit before I could even lay hands on her and pray; and she got up healed.

Do Stay focused on the Lord: It is my conviction that we need the power of God to conduct the healing ministry, and the ministry gifts and the enabling power flow out of our personal relationship with the Lord. When Martin Luther had extra work he needed done, he reportedly said that he needed to spend extra time in prayer in order to accomplish it. My personal time alone with the Lord has been my lifeline since 1976.

Jesus told us to learn from His example (Matthew 11:29; John 13:15), and He gives us a wonderful example of personal communion with the Father as well as how to cooperate with the Holy Spirit. The Gospel of Luke is a carefully researched book, and Luke tells us that Jesus *"would often slip away to the wilderness and pray"* (Luke 5:16). In Luke 6 we are told that Jesus spent the entire night in prayer (v. 12). I find it interesting that following these two passages we see evidence of a special anointing on the Lord for healing. One verse later, immediately after the Lord slips away to pray in the wilderness, we find that *"the power of the Lord was present for Him to perform healing"* (5:17). We are not sure of the elapsed time between verses 16 and 17, but we see the same phenomena again in Luke 6:12 and 19. Here it appears that the power to heal is present the very next day following a night of prayer.

Jesus said in John 10 that the sheep know the voice of their shepherd and they will follow him because they know his voice. This is the way it should be with us and the Lord. Having a regular personal time alone with the Lord allows us to begin to correctly discern His voice, and this gives Him the opportunity to take the initiative in our lives. It takes practice to learn to hear His voice, and we all mistake our own thoughts for His voice at times, but with perseverance we can begin to reliably know His voice.

Do Thank Him for What You See Him Doing: Many times we do not see the completed healing immediately after we have ministered, but often we see some improvement. Thank Him for the improvement. When we see improvement, we almost always see additional improvement the next time we pray. We need to be thankful for what we do see and expectant for additional healing. The healing of the brain tumor that was mentioned previously, occurred over three separate times of ministry.

Share testimonies with each other. Testimonies are encouraging to those ministering healing and are sign posts to lead others to a healing

God. Keep a record of healings you have seen and review them from time to time. These healing testimonies are a personal record of how God has used you in the past and will be an encouragement for the future. As the years go by, we tend to forget many of the healings we have witnessed. It is good to refresh our memories on how faithful God has been to us in this area.

Read the accounts of others who are used in healing. The writings and teachings of Randy Clark, Bill Johnson, Cal Pierce, John G. Lake, Francis MacNutt, Charles and Frances Hunter, Kathryn Kuhlman, John Wimber, T. L. Osborn, Maria Woodworth-Etter, William Branham, Ian Andrews, and Smith Wigglesworth—to name a few—all provide ample evidence and encouragement regarding God's healing today.

Do Keep a Regular Schedule of Prayer and Fasting: Jesus expects us to fast; He gave instructions about giving, praying, and fasting in Matthew 6. All three disciplines are rewarding. By and large, Christians in America have lost the sense of value and importance of fasting. This was not always the case. During the Civil War, President Lincoln, with the consent of the Senate, called "For a Day of National Humiliation, Fasting and Prayer." The Proclamation began by recognizing "the Supreme Authority and Just Government of Almighty God, in all the affairs of men and of nations." America has strayed so very far from this exercise in humility today but individuals still need to recognize this Supreme Authority in their own lives and seek His divine wisdom and initiative. Fasting helps us do this. Fasting does not change God or His will for us, but it does help us be more in tune to His desires and gives us inner strength to continue the fight against the darkness in this world. In Matthew's account of Jesus healing the epileptic son (Matthew 17:14-21), the disciples asked Jesus why they could not accomplish the healing and drive out the spirit involved. His response was, *"But this kind does not go out except by prayer and fasting"* (v. 21).

I personally prefer a regular schedule of fasting as opposed to living life without fasting which is then interrupted by extended periods of fasting. If fasting actually is a tool that assists us in our battle against evil spirits, I need to always be ready. I can't wait until I encounter a demon that needs to be removed to begin fasting; I need to be fasted and prayed up already. One thing I often do is omit my mid-day meal. I've noted that when God fed both the children of Israel and Elijah that he provided food morning and evening, not at noon. Also, inserting a fasting day or period into your weekly schedule seems advisable. A couple of good references on fasting are *Shaping History through Prayer & Fasting* by Derek Prince, and *The Rewards of Fasting* by Mike Bickle and Dana Candler.

Do Get Some Rest: Even Jesus knew the value of rest and relaxation as He invited His disciples to come away to a secluded place (Mark 6:31-32). The prophet Bob Jones once told us that sometimes the godliest thing you can do is take a nap. When we are tired, the spirit of discouragement is much more likely to be able to influence us than when we are rested. For those of us involved in the healing ministry, there are always needs to be met. Requests will come in for prayer from friends of sick people as well as those who are ill. Many of these requests will require travel time to a home or hospital room in addition to the ministry time itself. Jesus was open to doing this (Matthew 8:7) so we must be as well. However, the key is to be led by the Spirit; we are not Jesus and are not responsible for everyone's healing. If we focus on doing only our part, the grace for ministry will be there.

Let's finish this chapter with a recent story about how we were led, unknowingly, by the Spirit to minister healing to a woman who lives 950 miles away from Kansas City. Doris' brother had passed away, his remains were cremated, and his family was gathering at a reservoir in north-east Wyoming for a memorial time when his ashes were to be scattered in the lake where he often fished. The gathering included almost forty people and they occupied some camp sites near the marina with their campers, RVs, and tents. Doris and I tried, unsuccessfully, to make reservations near their camp site but eventually ended up almost 8 miles away with a room above a bait shop. When we checked into our room, the bait shop owner mentioned that there was a futon in our room which she had been unable to close because she had a "dead arm." We went about our family reunion that weekend and as we were leaving two days later, the Holy Spirit reminded Doris that our hostess had a "dead arm." We asked her nearby husband if he thought she would like us to pray for her; he asked that she probably would so we proceeded to the bait shop to ask her. She was also a follower of Jesus and willingly allowed us to pray. The Lord touched and healed her on the spot so we left on our return trip rejoicing that we had been instruments of the Lord for healing in a remote part of Wyoming.

PART II
DELIVERANCE

CHAPTER 9

Healing the Demonized

Deliverance is the process of someone being set free from the direct influence of evil spirits. By using the term "direct influence," I'm trying to differentiate between the influence evil spirits have on all of us because we live in a fallen world and the specific, or direct, influence that an evil spirit exercises to alter the way someone feels, thinks, or acts. There was a time when I did not believe in the literal, actual involvement of evil spirits in someone's life. I believed the Bible, of course, but I thought that the biblical authors were just explaining things the best way they knew how. Our modern world with all its advancements in science, medicine, and psychology should be able to describe things more accurately than to attribute some things to evil spirits. For example, instead of saying someone may have a spirit of fear or "*timidity*" as Paul does in 2 Timothy 1:7, in our current wisdom we could identify that person as being paranoid. Now that I have seen fearful people delivered of spirits of fear and paranoia, I don't think I am so smart anymore.

Many Christians are reluctant to get involved in the ministry of deliverance. I can understand that. Deliverance can be messy, tiring, misunderstood, and frustrating. It can also be very rewarding, and if I read my Bible correctly, it is part of the ministry that Jesus expects us to do on His behalf. Jesus clearly gave His disciples power and authority over demonic powers (see Luke 9 and 10), He commissioned all believers to conduct this ministry in Mark 16, and the early church followed these instructions (see Acts 5:16 and 8:7). Any born again believer can minister deliverance. Most of us did not become aware of the reality of demons until after we were filled with the Spirit, but this is not a requirement. First John 4:4 says, *"Greater is He who is in you than he who is in the world."* If you have Jesus in your heart, you have the power and authority to command evil spirits to leave someone.

You do, however, normally need the consent and agreement of the one needing deliverance. Let me share a couple of examples. Once I had a student come for deliverance ministry. Things were proceeding nicely, the Holy Spirit was identifying the evil spirits, we were commanding them to leave, and there were obvious manifestations as they exited. The Holy Spirit indicated that the student was involved with some drug abuse and named a spirit of marijuana. As I came against this spirit, the student exclaimed: "Hey, wait a minute. I like that. I didn't come here for that." So, we were done; the session was over. Bill Johnson reportedly once said, "We can have any spirit we want."

Another, very recent incident, concerns a young man I will call BJ. BJ has been in and out of mental facilities, and has been diagnosed as schizophrenic/bi-polar. I first visited him in the mental institution at his invitation and on the initiation of his father. He is very tormented by demons and is obsessed with religion, especially things recorded in the Book of Revelation, who is the beast, when will Jesus return, etc. He recently was discharged from the hospital and called and asked for ministry. I picked him up at his apartment and took him to Hope City where we used our healing room for a ministry time. I took him through the process of closing open doors, forgiveness for himself was a major issue—he just found out he was going to be a father, the woman he had sex with previously was six months pregnant and wants to keep the baby. I prepared him for what he might experience as I commanded spirits to leave; feeling something move inside, the possible need to cough, yawn, or take deep breaths. As we began to minister against spirits of rejection and fear, not much seemed to happen except some deeper breathing, and then as I continued, he started yawning as each spirit exited. I went back through some of the spirits I had already commanded to leave and we continued to get manifestations of the spirits leaving. Suddenly, he decided he wanted to quit so we shut down the session. He apparently was afraid of what was happening. I tried to explain what he was feeling and encouraged him to continue, but he was adamant about quitting. I do know the spirits were leaving and he knew it too as he could feel it; but he was in charge of the session and I did not want to try to force him to continue. My hope is that he will notice the difference, some freedom in his life, and will contact me for ministry in the future. If he does seek deliverance ministry again, I will want some assurance that he will follow through both during the session and after. As of this writing, he has not contacted me requesting additional ministry.

Conversely, when the person being ministered to is in agreement, much good can come from a deliverance session. Last year a pastor from a congregation here in Kansas City asked me to minister to a lady from her church. The woman was having a very difficult time; she had some major problems in her own life and in addition, her father was dying of AIDS. She was divorced and now remarried but struggled with her relationship largely due to previous lesbian encounters. She was tormented by demons in several areas of her life. The Lord set her free in about a two hour session. Along the way, He provided a word of knowledge about some severe pain she had and that issue was addressed as well. A couple of weeks later, I received this report from her pastor: "I wanted to tell you that Alice is beside herself with being pain-free and spirit-free! She has so much joy in her and is a blessing to whomever she is talking with!! PTL for His faithfulness!" Results like this make deliverance ministry a very rewarding undertaking.

What exactly are demons or evil spirits? The Bible does not specifically answer this question, and godly men and women disagree on the correct response. Many believe that demons represent the portion of angels that Satan took with him when he left heaven. It seems reasonable to expect these fallen angels to be active in serving their master, Satan, but it is not clear exactly what function they are performing now. They may be the spiritual forces in heavenly places that Paul speaks about in Ephesians 6:12, but they may represent more of the "officers" in Satan's army rather than the "privates," i.e., the demons that actually harass and invade our individual lives.

Demons are not spirits of the dead sent back to earth. They are definitely expressions of evil as they are connected to the primary evil being himself—Satan. They do seem to have a personality of sorts that constantly seeks to express itself by occupying a person and influencing their thoughts or deeds. They are "driven" compulsive beings that are compelled to exercise their evil influence on humans.

Can a Christian Have a Demon?

The tongue in cheek answer to this question, of course, is "who would want one?" However, this is one of the most frequently asked questions regarding deliverance that we receive from Christians, and they earnestly desire a correct answer. The body of Christ is divided on this issue, and as usual, godly men and women can disagree on the answer. Some Christian denominations have statements of doctrine which specifically deny the possibility that Christians can have demons. The Bible is not specific on the answer to this question, and we must give grace to others in the way that they interpret the Scriptures. I prefer to rephrase the question slightly and state it as: "Can a Christian be directly influenced by a demon?" In my opinion, the response to this question is clearly "yes."

Let's examine this issue in more detail. We generally have three ways to determine if something is doctrinally correct. The first and most sure way is if the Scriptures are very clear regarding the issue in question. If the answer can clearly be found in Scripture, the question is answered and no further discussion is needed. If Scripture is not definite, then we can look to the practice of the early church - those Christians only recently removed from the complete, verbal teachings of Jesus - to determine what their understanding was. And finally we look to our own experience and understanding.

First, let's see what Scripture reveals regarding Christians being influenced by demons. From 1 Corinthians 12:10, we see that the gift of distinguishing of spirits is one of the manifestations of the Spirit given to the church for the common good. As Paul discusses the use of the gifts in the context of being used *within* the body in the following chapters, it seems reasonable that he intended this gift to be used within the body also, i.e., amongst believers. However, it can be argued that Paul intended for this gift to be used for protection from *outside* the church and not from within.

In Mark 7:24-30 is the story of when Jesus delivers the daughter of the Syrophoenician woman from a demon. He also indicated in verse 27 that this deliverance represents the "children's bread," inferring that as a Gentile she was outside God's chosen people and that it was the Jews who had the right to expect this freedom. In Romans Paul argues that it is the children of promise who are the children of God (9:8), that there is now no distinction between Jew and Greek (10:12), and that the Gentiles have been grafted into God's kingdom (11:13, 17). If non-Jewish Christians use these scriptures to justify their acceptance to God for salvation and the other promises of the kingdom, should they not also be used to indicate that deliverance is available to them as well?

Some Christians would agree with the preceding paragraph but would say that the deliverance from evil was obtained through the atonement, and comes into the life of the believer as soon as he or she accepts Christ. Yet, if deliverance from evil spirits happens for all new believers, then what about sickness? Isaiah outlined one of the blessings of Christ's atonement to be freedom from sickness (Isaiah 53:4-5). This indeed is a fundamental scripture that encourages us to continue to pray for the sick, but none of us would (or should) call someone an unbeliever because they showed up in church ill! If a believer can't be influenced by an evil spirit, he certainly shouldn't be sick. In fact, we find just the opposite. We sometimes must deal with the spirit before the healing can occur. We should not be surprised by this, Jesus was not (Luke 13:11). If you desire to minister to the sick, you need to have some understanding regarding deliverance as you will not be able to minister to the sick very long before being confronted with a demon.

I believe that Scripture can speak to us on more than one level, and the story of Lazarus resurrection (John 11) speaks to me of deliverance from evil spirits for God's people. Looking at verses 43 and 44:

When He had said these things, He cried out with a loud voice, "Lazarus, come forth." He who had died came forth, bound hand and foot with wrappings; and his face was wrapped around with a cloth. Jesus said to them, "Unbind him, and let him go."

HEALING AND DELIVERANCE FUNDAMENTALS

We were dead in our trespasses and sins (Ephesians 2:1) when Jesus called to us, "Come forth. Come forth to life. Be born again." Even though we responded to His call and accepted Him as our Lord, becoming Christians, we were still in bondage. We needed help, i.e., deliverance. This deliverance from our sins, our habits, our past, or evil spirits can take several forms; but sometimes Jesus points out one of His people to us who is in bondage to evil spirits and says, "*Unbind him, and let him go.*"

The closest biblical reference to Christians being clearly influenced by a demon is found in Acts 4 and 5. In Acts 4, verses 32-35, Luke describes how the congregation of believers was of one heart and soul regarding their property, and how the *believers* would sell their land and bring the proceeds to the apostles for distribution as they saw fit. Three verses later (Acts 5:1-11), we find Ananias and Sapphira selling their property and bringing it to the apostles. The action of laying the proceeds at the apostles' feet is indicated in both Acts 4:35 and 5:2, so it should be safe to assume that Ananias and Sapphira were part of this congregation of believers.

Yet, as the story of Ananias and Sapphira unfolds, Peter states that they have been influenced by Satan. Scripture reveals that Satan uses demons to carry out his plans (See Ephesians 6:11ff and Luke 13:10-16). In the Luke 13 reference, the Bible plainly shows that Satan had bound the woman with a sickness for 18 years and he used a demon spirit to do it. If Satan uses demons to carry out his schemes, and the Bible indicates that he does, then it is reasonable to state that Ananias and Sapphira, both of whom were Christians, were being directly influenced by demons. If we had been given the opportunity to minister deliverance to these two, we likely would have encountered spirits of deception or lying along with others such as insecurity or fear of the future.

Another biblical reference on this issue can be found in 1 Timothy 4:1. In this verse Paul indicates the Holy Spirit has said that some believers will fall away from the faith because they were directly influenced by demons.

Secondly, the early church apparently practiced deliverance on Christians. One would assume that the early church would have an accurate understanding of whether new believers could still be directly influenced by demons. Dr. Francis MacNutt, in his book *Deliverance from Evil Spirits* (p. 134), discusses a third-century church practice which clearly indicates that exorcism (deliverance) was to be made available to baptized church members. Presumably these baptized church members were believing Christians. MacNutt states:

> Notice that the Church acknowledged the possibility of baptized persons needing exorcism, in contrast to the common belief held today (in Pentecostal churches and elsewhere) that no Christian can possibly need deliverance, only pagans.

And finally, our personal experience bears abundant witness to the truth that many Christians have been influenced by demons. I can attest to this from my own life as the Lord graciously set me free from a habitual sin by delivering me from an evil spirit. I was a spirit-filled Christian who regularly exercised spiritual gifts, but I still had an area of my own life with which I was fighting a losing battle. As I felt that spirit leave me, I knew the victory had been won - and it had. I thank the Lord for his goodness in revealing the thing that was hindering my walk with Him. The fruit that deliverance has borne in the lives of most of the Christians to whom we have ministered is ample evidence that something positive happened when together we resisted the presence of the evil within and/or around them.

When deliverance of Christians is viewed through the theological lens proposed years ago by Jonathan Edwards; i.e., does the activity (1) bring honor to the name of Jesus, (2) produce hatred for sin or love for righteousness, (3) produce a greater regard for Scripture, (4) lead people into the truth, or (5) produce greater love for God and man; if we can answer positively to any one of these five items, then we must conclude that it is the Holy Spirit not Satan who has initiated this activity. Satan cannot, or would not if he could, cause any one of these five fruits to occur. We have ministered deliverance to Christians for over twenty years and the evidence of these fruits in their lives gives us no choice but to continue to minister even if we are sometimes misunderstood by our brothers and sisters in Christ. In fact, we are very reluctant to minister deliverance to anyone who is *not* a professing Christian and would only do this under very special circumstances. If someone seeking deliverance is not a Christian, there is a high probability that even if delivered they would not be able to keep their house clean (see Matthew 12:43-45).

Some Christians want to deny the validity of any experience and state that only what is written in the word can be used as a basis of faith. However, did not the early church trust in their spiritual experiences? The outpouring of the Holy Spirit in Acts 2 was the evidence that Peter needed to associate the words of the prophet Joel with their experience:

> *Even upon My bondslaves, both men and women, I will in those days pour forth of My Spirit And they shall prophesy* (Acts 2:18).

I don't mean to imply that we should equate our experiences with the truth of Scripture, but I do believe that godly people can be guided by the Holy Spirit into experiences that help us interpret what God is saying and even doing in the present time. Actually, we can't even be saved without *experiencing* Jesus in our lives. It is not enough to know *about* Him, we must *know* Him. When we seek to determine if someone is a believer of not, we do not say, "Have you read the Bible?" Instead we say, "Do you know the Lord?"

If this section of the book has disturbed you, please make it a matter of prayer and let the Holy Spirit help you with the answer. Jesus said that He would send us the Spirit - which He did - and that the Spirit would guide us into all the truth (John 16:13). Let Him do that for you on this issue. It is not a question of whose theology is correct; I'm sure that the Lord will straighten me out on several points when I get to heaven. I just hate to see Christians denied help because they do not consider deliverance as a possible solution to their problem. Everything is not caused by an evil spirit, obviously; but some things are and we need to be aware of that possibility. The Lord spoke a convicting sentence to me once. He said: "I am tired of the enemy glorying in the fact that he can put something on my people when I died to set them free."

This sentence is an on-going reminder of a necessary area of ministry with which I am to be involved.

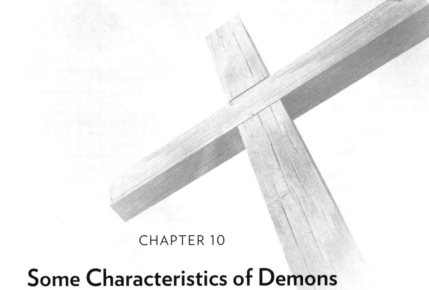

CHAPTER 10

Some Characteristics of Demons

The 12th chapter of Matthew contains a teaching of Jesus that gives some good in-sights into the characteristics of demons. Let's look at Matthew 12:43-45:

> *Now when the unclean spirit goes out of a man, it passes through waterless places, seeking rest, and does not find it. Then it says, "I will return to my house from which I came"; and when it comes, it finds it unoccupied, swept, and put in order. Then it goes, and takes along with it seven other spirits more wicked than itself, and they go in and live there; and the last state of that man becomes worse than the first. That is the way it will also be with this evil generation.*

From this scripture, we see that evil spirits have a will. The spirit said, "*I **will** return*"; and it did. It decided to do something. Thus, a spirit may decide to influence the life of person A but not to try to influence the life of person B. This is interesting food for thought. If person B has a strong walk with the Lord and is seeking to serve God, it may be more difficult for an evil spirit to influence the life of person B. Presumably the spirit will get the same gratification from being involved with either A or B, so he will likely choose the path of least resistance. This possibility alone should be a continual reminder for us to engage in the normal spiritual activities of Bible study, prayer, and worship.

Secondly, we see that the spirit desires a body, a person, with which it can express its personality. It is uncomfortable without a person; it is not at "rest." I don't believe that evil spirits are ever completely at rest, only those of us who know Jesus as Lord can experience His joy, rest, and peace. However, they apparently are a driven lot; and they get some sort of gratification from exercising their personality through a human.

We also understand that demonic spirits seem to be more secure with other evil spirits than if they are alone. They become stronger as part of a company of evil spirits, some more powerful or wicked than they. We observe this when we minister deliverance. Seldom do we see someone with only one demon, and some of the evil spirits are definitely stronger than others. In fact, if we can break up the stronghold and expel the primary demon; the rest of the deliverance generally goes much quicker and easier.

In Mark 5:1-14, the story of the Gerasene demoniac, we see that demons sometimes have the ability to speak through someone. We have seen this happen on several occasions, but it is not a regular occurrence. John Wimber tells of an encounter of this nature during the first time he ministered deliverance. As he approached the pickup truck where a young couple from his congregation was awaiting his arrival, the young woman stuck her head out of the window and in an unusual voice shouted, "I know who you are." John remembers thinking that at that moment he didn't want her to know who he was.

I have had similar experiences where the spirit will speak though someone and say something like, "Why did you have to come," or, "I'm going to kill you." It sounds exciting, but it really isn't. I normally pay very little attention to what evil spirits say, and I am not in the habit, as some are, of trying to extract information from them through conversation. They are liars by nature anyway (John 8:44), so I much prefer to get my information from the Holy Spirit who leads us into all the truth.

Evil spirits may cause a person to get upset or angry during ministry, but don't be afraid of them. I once was doing deliverance on a young man who rushed at me from across the room as an evil spirit manifested and took momentary control of him. I was sitting on the edge of my desk, and didn't move as he came at me. Before he reached me, he changed his direction and instead began beating his head against the wall. Jesus had the ultimate victory that day as well.

Some Characteristics of Demons

The passage in Mark also reveals that the demons exhibit self-awareness and an awareness of each other and their surroundings. In verse 9, the primary demon tells Jesus that *my* name is Legion, and it also tells Jesus of the presence of many other spirits. In verse 12, we see that they are aware that there are swine in the area as they ask Jesus for permission to enter the swine. From this passage we also see that demons can sometimes inhabit animals although their main desire is to be able to express their personality through humans.

Although we never should feel any sort of pity or sympathy toward a demon, they do exhibit emotions of their own. For example, in Mark 5:5 they caused the demoniac to cry out constantly and in verse 12 they pleaded with Jesus on their own behalf. Demons will sometimes attempt to make the deliverance minister feel sorry for them in the hope that they will be allowed to remain where they are. I remember on one occasion as we neared the end of a lengthy deliverance session that the remaining spirit complained that he was all alone. He too was quickly made to leave.

Activities of Demons

The Bible gives us many indications of activities in which evil spirits engage. Although it is not an exhaustive list, some of the more common activities are shown in Table 2 below.

Table 2: Activities of Demons

ACTIVITY	REFERENCE
They entice and tempt	1 Cor. 7:5; James 1:13-14
They deceive	1 Timothy 4:12
They enslave	Romans 8:15; 2 Pet. 2:19-20; John 8:34
Cause fear, timidity	2 Tim. 1:7; 1 John 4:18
They defile	Titus 1:15
They teach	1 Tim. 4:1
They cause illness	Luke 13:11
They do the works of Satan	Luke 11:17-19; John 8:38-41, 44
They lie	John 4:44

We don't need to be concerned about these activities, only aware of them. The more we know of the enemy's tactics, the better equipped we are to minister to those whom he influences and resist his attempts to influence us.

CHAPTER 11

A Typical Deliverance Session

No two sessions are alike, and we never want to get into a rut about how to minister to someone. The Holy Spirit is our guide and He can direct us to omit something we normally would do or to proceed in a certain way that we may never have done before. It is good, however, to have a general outline of how to proceed; and I offer here a general format that has proved productive for us many times.

First: Close the Open Doors

Demons operate under the Biblical rule book, and they have a reason why they are active in somebody's life. Unless the spiritual right for the evil spirit to influence someone is removed, deliverance is normally not successful or lasting; and it is actually unwise to attempt. Let me be quick to say, however, that the demonized individual *may not* be responsible for the reason or, in some cases, they may not even be aware of the reason. In other words, don't be too quick to judge or condemn the person you are ministering to. Remember Paul's admonition to the Corinthians, "*Let all that you do be done in love*" (1 Corinthians 16:14). It is our understanding that an entry point for a demon normally takes the form of one of the following:

Sin
Spiritual Adultery
Unforgiveness

Trauma

Curse

Sin: Deliberate, rebellious, repetitive sin is an open door for demonic access. We all sin, of course, and we certainly fall short of the glory of God. However, when we repeatedly and intentionally disobey God's law and His desire for our lives; we are in a state of rebellion and are prey for the evil one. When we find sin to be the cause of demonic activity, we seek to lead the individual into serious repentance and have them get their lives back on track with their Creator.

It is surprising sometimes how double minded we humans can be. We want the Lord to be active in our lives, yet we do not want to give up our selfish desires and sinful pleasures which separate us from Him (Isaiah 59:2). James writes that a double-minded man is unstable in all his ways (James 1:8). We become double minded when our mind is not in agreement with the Lord's.

Spiritual Adultery: We designate an activity as spiritual adultery when someone seeks a supernatural experience apart from those initiated by the Holy Spirit. These activities may take the form of experimenting with an Ouija board, séances, black magic, witchcraft, transcendental meditation, eastern religions, satanic cults, drugs, new age activities, etc. Any time that we willingly expose ourselves to activities that are sponsored by Satan we are in dangerous waters. Closing this open door is a matter of having the person renounce their involvement in any illegal activity followed by verbalizing their desire to have the Lord as their spiritual source. We feel it is important for this confession to be made out loud so there are witnesses, and so the spiritual world has no doubt regarding where loyalties lie.

I once had a graduate student who was not a believer and had been engaged in mind control. He was very accomplished in his ability to influence others but began to experience mental difficulty himself. He told me one day that he had lost control of his life. He would have periods of several hours that he would not have any understanding of what he had done or where he had been. He was seeing a mental health professional but was very concerned and confused over this turn of events. I shared the Lord with him and expressed the thought that he had opened himself up to demonic oppression and that he needed deliverance. He was desperate and open to anything that might help. I arranged for a team of believers to pray for him. Before ministering we shared the Lord with him in more detail and were convinced that he had truly repented of his activities and had accepted the saving grace of God in his life. The deliverance session itself was not very dramatic but the change in my student's life was.

Participating in the martial arts can, in my opinion, lead to an open door for demonic oppression. We have experienced this on more than one occasion. Recently we had a student at the Grace Training Center from Germany and she shared with us about her experience with Tae Kwon Do. At the time she began participating in Tae Kwon Do, neither she nor her instructor were Christians. Her instructor later became a Christian and began researching the roots of the sport. He discovered that it came from Zen-Buddhism and that "Do" meant spirit. She also noticed that some of the better Korean black belts would spend time in meditation before warming up for the fight. Her instructor had struggled with anger consistently before meeting with his pastor for prayer during which the bondage to Tae Kwon Do was cut. The difference in the instructor's behavior was noticed by the students without knowing what he had done, and he soon stopped his involvement with this activity.

Don't underestimate how clever and subtle the enemy is in his ability to entrap people in this area. He doesn't blatantly identify his activities but draws people into participating in unclean conduct that can lead to demonization. The following story of a twelve-year-old boy is true except his name has been changed to avoid his identification.

> In March of this year, Sam, a young man about twelve years old, came to where we were conducting a public healing service with a very serious issue. His entire family came up for prayer with him. He had severe stomach pain that came like a punch in the stomach at regular intervals. The pain was so serious he had been unable to attend school for two weeks. We prayed without any noticeable results. Then, we discerned that the root cause was a spirit and commanded the spirit to leave. There was an obvious manifestation as the spirit left and Sam said, "I feel good," and there were smiles all around.

The following week, I received a call while at home from Sam's father. He indicated that the relief Sam had experienced only lasted for about 15 minutes and then the pain was back. He asked if he could make an appointment with us to pray again for Sam when they came to Kansas City; they had made an appointment with a specialist for further physical examination. Of course, we said yes, and began to pray about the upcoming meeting. Because Sam had received immediate relief when I commanded the spirit behind the pain to leave, I was convinced it was a spiritual issue but needed to find its entry point and why it felt it had the right to continue harassing Sam. As I prayed over this issue, the Lord revealed that the source and entry point for the spirit was involvement with Harry Potter books.

When we met with the Sam and his parents, I asked Sam if he liked to read. He said no and his parents laughed at this suggestion. But then he spoke up and said what he did like to read, and was drawn to, was the Harry Potter book series. He also watches the movies that were made based on the Potter books. In fact, he said he watched them "all the time." His mother said she had taken to reading him the books now as he was so distressed and in pain much of the time so he was unable to read them himself. I explained that the Lord had indicated that this was the entry point and if he would agree to get rid of the books and movies, he could be set free. He immediately reacted strongly in a negative way and said "I can't give them up!!" His reaction was so strong that I presume this was the spirit talking through Sam. Sam got physically agitated when his father suggested that if he did give the books and movies up that perhaps he could be well. He got up and left the room and ran outside the building and he would not return. He wasn't willing to give these up, and currently that's where it stands.

Sam's family will likely seek additional medical testing, but it probably won't get them what they desire. Although Sam belonged to a serious Christian family, they were unaware of spiritual consequences of activities that promoted witchcraft. They viewed the books and movies as harmless childhood fantasy. So unless Sam

A Typical Deliverance Session

decides he is willing to renounce his involvement, actually worship of the Harry Potter material, he will probably continue to have difficulties. I do not fault the parents; our society has promoted these commodities for children's entertainment and for the most part, our churches are silent on these issues. In Sam's case, it went beyond casual involvement to where it approached worship.

Unforgiveness: Unforgiveness is a sin, of course, but we always cover this open door specifically. Unforgiveness and bitterness towards people who have hurt us are so common in the body of Christ that many of us accept them as part of life and do not label them as the sins they really are. Forgiving is often difficult, especially when there is a legitimate reason for the unforgiveness, i.e., someone has actually sinned against another. This can take many forms including verbal, physical, or sexual abuse; desertion; slander; cheating, etc. We almost always use the story Jesus told in Matthew 18 about the king with the servant who owed him the large debt. This story makes it clear that the debt owed us is small in comparison to the debt the Lord has already forgiven us, and that we are to forgive someone even though they actually owe us a debt. The story also makes it clear that if we do not forgive, the Lord Himself will turn us over to the tormentors, torturers, or jailers—however your particular version reads. This torment or torture often comes in the form of a demonic messenger who desires to make life miserable.

The key to closing the open door of unforgiveness is to forgive the one involved and to cancel the debt they owe you. This is often much easier said than done and it may take some time to work through these issues prior to beginning any deliverance. Dr. Sam Storms, a former Associate Professor at Wheaton College, teaches that there are five myths surrounding forgiveness. He teaches that:

Forgiveness does not suggest that you must completely forget.

It does not mean that you no longer feel the pain associated with the event.

It does not require us to cease asking for justice. (We must let God be the author of the justice, however.)

We do not have to make it easy for the person to hurt us again.

Forgiveness is seldom a one time event.

We have seen the issue of forgiving someone unlock physical and demonic strongholds. We once ministered to a woman who had been paralyzed from the slip of a surgeon's knife during an operation. As she agreed to forgive the doctor involved, her paralyzed arm began to vibrate without anyone laying hands on her, and she obtained substantially more movement and control immediately. We also ministered deliverance to a student who was emotionally bound from a disappointing romantic relationship. Even though he mentally agreed with us after we shared the importance of forgiving the young lady involved, he had great difficulty in actually speaking the words of forgiveness. The simple sentence of "I forgive Jane" became an ordeal that took over an hour to work through. Each time he attempted to speak that sentence, the spirits involved would resist him in a powerful way. Finally, after considerable prayer and effort, he was able to fully release the young lady and speak the words. This act broke the power of the enemy in his life and deliverance followed.

We all know that we can harbor unforgiveness towards others, but we can have difficulty forgiving ourselves and God as well. We may ask the Lord to forgive us for something we have done and believe that he has forgiven, but still hold ourselves accountable in some way. When we don't forgive ourselves, in essence we are denying that the blood of Jesus was sufficient for our sin. We are actually saying that we can only be forgiven if *we do* something as well. We know this is not theologically correct, but many times a breakthrough comes in a deliverance session only after the person being ministered to forgives themselves.

We must also sometimes forgive God. The Lord hasn't sinned or done anything wrong, of course, but as humans we sometimes hold Him responsible for tragic things that happen to us and around us. It wasn't God's desire that our parents divorced or that our best friend died from cancer. These issues are difficult and beyond the scope of this book, but we must continue to recognize that things happen here on earth that are not the Lord's first desire for us. Reading 1 Timothy 2:4 helps us understand this issue.

A Typical Deliverance Session

Trauma: The enemy does not play fair and even small children are subject to influence from demons because of traumatic events that happen to them. For example, a child that watches a horror movie on TV may become open to a spirit of fear, or an unwanted child may receive a spirit of rejection at a very early age. We will discuss ministering to children in more detail in the next chapter.

Adults as well may receive spiritual baggage because of trauma in their lives. Trauma can originate through a physical experience such as an automobile accident or a difficult surgery, or it can be an emotional event as well. Perhaps you went through a difficult divorce and although innocent of any wrong doing, you now suffer from guilt and rejection. Both of these emotional responses may be real, but frequently the enemy takes advantage of the situation to initiate the influence of a spirit of guilt and a spirit of rejection. We need discernment in order to know the difference. We can't cast out an emotion that needs healing, but we will never be completely healed if we need deliverance from a spirit that is coupled to the wound.

I recently ministered to a Christian lady whose husband had left her for another woman. The emotional turmoil that the situation had generated in her life had left her open to spiritual attack. She was delivered of spirits of fear and anxiety among others. Inner healing is a key part of being able to keep free in cases like these. When someone has to live in a situation that caused the open door to occur initially, they need a solid support system. The enemy knows the weak areas in our lives and he will exploit them if at all possible.

Curses: The subject of curses is far too broad to discuss in detail here, and the interested reader is referred to Derrick Prince's book entitled: "Blessing or Curse." Curses are real and can either be generational, having been passed down through the blood line, or they can be specific curses hurled against someone as an act of witchcraft or black magic, etc. Spiritual discernment in identifying the curse is essential, and the curse can be broken by the minister exercising his authority in the name of Jesus.

For generational curses, I frequently remind the believer, and the spirit world, that the believer has a new blood line from the lineage of Jesus and he or she is no longer bound by the actions of their ancestors. We normally break the curse into past generations and proclaim that it cannot come forward onto the person's children or their children's children. Only occasionally do we see any outward physical manifestations when we are lead to break a curse, but we have been privileged to see fruit from this activity. We once broke a generational curse of asthma over a mother who was attending one of our conferences and she had a nine year old son at home who also suffered from this illness. After returning home, she discovered that not only was she free from this ailment, but her son had been set free also. Isn't God wonderful?

I also recently ministered to a couple who were having difficulty at home, and in the course of discussing their issues they mentioned that there had been family activity with the Masons on the husband's side. The husband was not sure if this was important or not and he also wasn't too sure about whether deliverance was a real experience for Christians. The Lord led me to break any curses over his family which evolved from the Masons and he was soon on his hands and knees on the floor being delivered from the effects of this demonic organization. It is so important to follow the leading of the Holy Spirit as we minister deliverance.

Second: Command the Spirits to Leave

Believing Christians have the power and authority to drive out evil spirits - once the doorways have been closed. First John 4:4 says, *"Greater is He who is in you than he who is in the world."* This is so absolutely true, but then, so is the rest of Scripture. It is necessary to renounce demonic activity as stated previously, but the second step is commanding the evil spirit(s) to leave. For example, there are printed prayers that are used by counselors and prayer ministers to break generational curses from secret organizations such as the Masonic Lodge. We normally have not found it necessary to use these detailed, printed prayers, but other ministers who use them indicate they have borne much fruit in the lives of those receiving ministry. However on occasion, the rituals themselves have attached spirits which must be expelled as well as renounced. For instance, I recently was in a ministry session where a woman read a printed prayer to receive freedom from the Scottish Rite. Parts of the prayer are repeated here, in part:

> ...of the Perfect Master Degree, its secret password of MAH-HAH-BONE, and its penalty of being smitten to the Earth with

A Typical Deliverance Session

a setting maul;...of the Provost and Judge Degree, its secret password of HIRUM-TITO-KY, and the penalty of having my nose cut off; ...of the Intendant of the Building degree, of its secret password AKAR-JAI-JAH, and the penalty of having my eyes put out, my body cut in two...

As she read the prayer, the Holy Spirit revealed that the passwords used in this rite were actual names of spirits. As the initiates repeated the oath, they actually were inviting spirits with these names into their lives. Using the password as names, each spirit was addressed and commanded to leave. There was an obvious physical reaction during the deliverance as each individual spirit left.

Start where your faith level is, and let the Lord build on it from there. For example, although Jesus could deliver a person from all their spirits with a single word, I simply have not seen that happen for me and I do not have the faith for it. However, I do have faith to command spirits of fear, lust, deception, etc. to leave; and so I do them as the Spirit identifies them. One by one we command the spirits to leave until we have a witness from the Holy Spirit that the work is done.

This approach may mean that the person will not be completely set free in a single session. When we first ministered deliverance, we would try to be sure that freedom came in a single encounter. After experiencing sessions that lasted for several hours, and sometimes into the early hours of the next day; we decided this was not either wise or necessary. Ministering draws from the spiritual resources of the minister, and it is not fair to either the minister or the person receiving ministry to conduct this activity at a low spiritual level. Generally people needing deliverance did not get to that state in the last few hours, and they are able to return at a later time for additional help.

Some manifestations may occur as the spirits leave. We are not surprised at this, as Jesus experienced the same (Mark 1:26). We do not look for physical manifestations, but we do not get concerned when they come. Generally, physical manifestations that do occur are mild and take the form of sighs, yawns, shaking, etc. However at other times, more intense physical activity can arise. These latter instances seem to be more prevalent when the individual has been involved in an occult activity either willingly or from an abusive situation such as during Satanic Ritual Abuse.

Third: Inner Healing

Many times inner healing needs to be a part of the deliverance ministry in order for the person Jesus sets free to remain free. John Wimber describes inner healing as "the process in which the Holy Spirit brings forgiveness of sin and emotional renewal to people suffering from damaged minds, wills, and emotions." Inner wounds are frequently where the enemy attacks to gain entrance. Unless deliverance is coupled with inner healing, keeping free from demonic influence may be unnecessarily difficult.

Some people who minister deliverance have found that it is to their advantage to minister inner healing before attempting any deliverance. If we use the analogy of a thorn piercing the flesh and causing a wound, those who minister deliverance prior to conducting inner healing view it as similar to pulling the thorn out so the flesh can heal unhindered. However, others have had good success ministering to the wound first and then finding that the thorn seems to fall gently out without much difficulty and sometimes on its own. As we have said before, it is important to cooperate with the Holy Spirit in these matters. You may be lead to minister deliverance first on some occasions and inner healing first on others. We try to be open to either but must confess that if we are left to our own methods, we are more prone to go after the thorns first.

God is active in inner healing. The psalmist tells us: "*Praise the* LORD.... *The* LORD *gathers the outcasts of Israel. He heals the brokenhearted, And binds up their wounds.*" (Psalm 147:1-3). Paul tells us in Romans 12:2 that we are to "*be transformed by the renewing of your mind.*"

Inner healing is difficult to describe, but the fruit is self evident. A major result of inner healing should be peace. No longer should there be inner torment, confusion, anxiety, etc. Inner healing can take place through many different avenues such as prayer, prayer in the Spirit, singing in the Spirit, etc. The Sanfords have a recent book which addresses this subject entitled *Deliverance and Inner Healing*. Another book, which we like on this topic, is Betty Tapsott's *Inner Healing Through the Healing of Memories*.

Fourth: Follow-up

There are several "dos" and "don'ts" that we recommend to the folks that come to us for deliverance. You can never force someone to follow these suggestions, but we have learned that those that disregard them may experience additional problems.

DO:

1. **Stay close to the Lord**. We suggest getting into a Christian fellowship. The body of believers is God's support agency. If you do not worship regularly with the body of Christ, you should do so. Consider joining a home group for support.

2. **Study God's Word**. St. Paul writes that we need the full armor of God to stand firm against the schemes of the devil (Ephesians 6:10-17). The offensive weapon he lists is the Word of God. Study the Bible. Ask the Holy Spirit, the author, to quicken it to your heart so that you may understand. Jesus quoted scripture in dealing with the enemy, and so can we (Luke 4:1-13).

3. **Spend time with God**. Pray for your needs and the needs of others. Ask the Lord to heal the memories that you may have of painful situations. Pray in the Spirit. God will continue to heal your hurts and memories as you pray in tongues (Ephesians 6:18; Romans 8:26). One Christian teacher says that we have to pray in tongues because we are not smart enough on our own to ask for everything we need in our native language.

4. **Praise God**. Praise is something God commands us to do, and it is a powerful tool. James 4:7 says, *"Submit therefore to God. Resist the devil and he will flee from you."* Praise goes before the battle. Read 2 Chronicles 20. When the people praised God, He went before them and destroyed their enemy. Often we do not feel like singing and praising God, but when we do it anyway

out of obedience, it isn't long before praise and joy bubble up spontaneously. Praising God is not just for God's sake; like all things that He requires of us, it is for our own well being also.

DON'T:

1. **Don't be afraid**. Christians do not need to fear picking up unclean spirits. You are protected by the helmet of salvation and the precious blood of Jesus. Satan has lost his legal right to live in your house. He has been evicted so he knows he is an unwanted trespasser. He may test you and seek to regain entrance, but he cannot enter a house that has been filled with the Holy Spirit unless you allow him to do so. You have put up a sign that says NO VACANCY!

2. **Don't abide in sin**. We all are prone to sin daily (1 John 1:8), and we fall short of the glory of God, but as we yield to the Lord and confess our sin; we are washed clean and are righteous before God (v. 9). Don't keep resentments against others, yourself, or God (Matthew 6:14-15).

3. **Don't choose to keep bad habits**. God may desire to change your lifestyle or circumstances to save you from temptation or spiritual conflict. Seek Him on this. (See 1 Corinthians 5:9-11 and 2 Corinthians 6:14-18.)

4. **Don't fear being tested**. God allows Satan to test us not so we will fall, but to show us how strong the Lord can be in our lives. Jesus loves you; He will not allow the enemy to snatch you out of His hand. (John 10:29).

Miscellaneous Comments

Deliverance is not a cure all. We still need to exercise the normal Christian disciplines that we all know about; praying, studying the scriptures, and

A Typical Deliverance Session

staying in fellowship with other believers. The Lord is always ready to help us, but we must exercise some self discipline of our own.

Many times we are unable to complete what needs to be done in a single session. That's okay. It is better to minister for a reasonable period of time and then schedule subsequent sessions until both the minister and the one receiving ministry are satisfied with the progress. It also is not unusual for someone who has received deliverance ministry to come back a month or six months later for additional ministry. Perhaps if the church was walking in its full role in holiness and righteousness we would see complete freedom come to individuals in a single session or in a single moment of time. However, the church isn't there yet and neither are any deliverance ministers that I know about; and consequently we still lack complete understanding, knowledge, authority, and power.

Ministering deliverance can be a difficult ministry. It is often misunderstood and shunned by other Christians. However, it is a very rewarding ministry. I encourage you to be open to the Lord leading you to minister in this area. As Mike Bickle, founder of the International House of Prayer in Kansas City, has said, "Seek to be worshipers of God and deliverers of men."

The deliverance ministry is normally a hidden ministry. People will reveal their innermost problems and sins, and the deliverance minister needs to be able to keep this information confidential. Occasionally we minister deliverance in a small group setting, but there needs to be an element of trust developed before most people would agree to allow themselves to be ministered to in this fashion.

Expect to have some failures. We have! I'm not sure why a spirit does not always leave. I have some ideas, but for now they will remain my own. In any event, I know that I have sometimes done everything that I know to do and the desired freedom has not come.

Let's close this chapter with a deliverance testimony:

> Bob was brought for ministry having just been released from a mental health facility. He was depressed, suicidal, very confused, and unable to distinguish reality from unreality. He was on some prescription anti-depression medication. He struggled with what was real and what was not. He said he would sometimes fondle

furniture or other items just to know by touch if they were real or not. He had a history of depression, but was also a very successful marketer. He was unsure what triggered this current episode. One major clue was that he was living out of wedlock with a woman who was a practicing Buddhist.

As we ministered, the spirits manifested and spoke to us often. A spirit of suicide pointed to the scar on his arm where he had cut himself and declared, "We did that." We silenced the spirits when they spoke and commanded them to go. There were obvious manifestations as the spirits left. One stubborn spirit was told to "go to the pit" by the person helping me, which I never do as I do not see scriptural evidence for this command. However, this particular spirit did scream as he departed so it may be honored by the Spirit in some instances. Another spoke out, "I hate you," as it left. This type of statement is not uncommon.

Bob appeared free and was lighter and happy when the ministry session was over. However, by the next day, he was having trouble again and needed additional ministry. Another key factor was when the Spirit revealed a major spirit with the name, "Eidolon." Eidolon is a synonym for a figment of the imagination, which was causing major issues in Bob's life. Removing this spirit was a huge step in his recovery. Bob has received additional ministry and on-going counsel and remains free from his depression.

CHAPTER 12

Ministering Deliverance to Children

The Gospels give us several examples of Jesus ministering to children. As we explore these examples, they will provide guidance for us as we seek to pray for ill or demonized children. When I speak of a young child in this chapter, it means a child that has not yet reached the age where he or she acts independently from his or her parents in making decisions. The age where ministry without the child's consent is not appropriate or feasible is not a definite, set age for each child. If a child exercises considerable independence in their lives; they, not the parent, must seek the ministry for themselves. Examples of independence would be setting their own schedule for bedtime or meals, driving the car alone, how they spend their time, or who they associate with, etc.

Biblical Examples

The Gospels list six examples of Jesus ministering to children. In three of these examples, the child is present. Let's look at these first.

In Mark 10:13-16, we see the love and compassion that Jesus has for children as He rebuked His disciples for not letting children come near Him. We will do well to always remember that our Lord said that to "*such as these*" belongs the Kingdom of God. This is the same kingdom that includes healing, deliverance, righteousness, peace, and joy (Luke 9; 10; Matthew 10; Romans 14:17). Although it is not specifically stated as such, apparently the children were brought to Jesus by someone who had physical, and thus spiritual, authority over them. Verse 13 mentions that "***they were bringing children to Him***" (emphasis added). In this encounter, Jesus takes the time to touch children and to bless them. We will do well to do the same with the little ones around us.

In the second example where Jesus ministers to a child that is present (Mark 9:14-29), the child's father brings his son while asking that he be set free from an evil spirit which makes his son mute and causes seizures, presumably from epilepsy. Notice that the son is no longer a young child; as upon being questioned, his father said that his condition had continued "from childhood." Since the son is no longer a young child, he may have reached the age where his consent was needed before Jesus could minister to him. In any event, the son did accompany his father and apparently did not lose physical control of himself until after Jesus rebuked the evil spirit. Another indication that the child, in this case, was willing to be ministered to by Jesus, is that the father appeals to Jesus on behalf of both of them (v. 22). It is not simply a father's request, but it is the son's request also.

We can identify several interesting and important concepts from this encounter between Jesus, his disciples, the father, and the epileptic son.

- Demons can inhabit or influence even a young child. The son had his difficulties from childhood.
- Jesus expected his disciples to be able to minister to this young man. From this we can surmise that we should be prepared to minister to children as well.
- Older children probably should be present to receive ministry as they need to give their consent.
- It was the father who asked Jesus for help, but apparently the son added his consent and was willing to receive prayer.
- Our prayer life is an important key which helps equip us to do the work of the ministry.

The third instance where a child is present when receiving ministry is found in Mark 5:22ff, Matthew 9:18ff, and Luke 8:41ff. Here a synagogue official, Jairus, comes to ask Jesus to come heal his dying daughter, but she dies while her father is seeking the Lord's help. Matthew's account differs from that recorded in Mark and Luke in that he writes that the daughter was already dead when Jairus spoke to Jesus. In any event, the daughter was in no position to seek help herself, and her father has exercised his parental authority on her behalf by asking Jesus to intervene. In this instance, we know that the daughter is twelve years old.

We shall now look at three biblical examples in which the child is absent. Note that in all of these remaining examples, the child is apparently a young child. I personally believe that the Lord allows younger children to receive ministry without being present to avoid any additional trauma that the ministry may inflict. They were not old enough to be spiritually accountable or to have given legal consent to the evil spirits, so the Lord sets them free with little fanfare.

The first of these examples where the child is not present during ministry is found in Matthew 8:5-13. Here we find a centurion's servant paralyzed and in a great deal of pain. Obviously an accident of some kind must have befallen this servant because if he had been paralyzed from birth, he could not ever have performed his duties to the centurion. We see from the note in the margin of the NASB (v. 6) and from the Amplified Bible that the servant is a young boy, or servant boy. Jesus heals the young servant boy without ever seeing or touching him. In this example, the centurion has legal, physical custody of the boy, and hence he had the spiritual authority to ask for his healing as well.

In the second example where the child is absent, a Gentile woman asks for the healing of her daughter who was plagued by an unclean spirit (Mark 7:25-30). Jesus frees the young child from the demon while the daughter is still at home. We know from verse 25 that the daughter is young as she is identified as the woman's "*little daughter.*" Because the young child is the woman's daughter, the mother has the spiritual authority to ask Jesus for the deliverance. An interesting side note here is that Jesus refers to deliverance as being the children's bread, i.e., His children are entitled to it.

In our last example, which is found in John 4:46-53, a father requests Jesus to heal his son of an illness which had brought him close to death. As before, the father has the physical custody of his child and therefore has the spiritual authority to ask for his healing. Jesus heals the son without physically going to him.

Personal Experiences

We frequently minister healing to children, even young children, by simply laying our hands on them and asking the Lord to touch them. We never would want to upset a child during ministry and some children are not open to strangers touching them. If this is the case, we just pray quietly in a conversational manner while a parent holds them. We have seen many positive results from such sessions. In the case of a young child, we would seldom minister deliverance while they are present just in case the spirits cause manifestations that would upset the child. We normally minister deliverance to young children with one or both parents present, as Jesus did in Mark 7, but without ministering directly to the child.

Autism is a disorder sometimes diagnosed in small children that are fascinated by repetitive activities or motion, do not show normal social interaction, and have communication issues. I am not an expert on autism, but we have had two children with this diagnosis set free through deliverance. One example of this sort of ministry occurred when the parents brought their son, who had been diagnosed with autism, to me for ministry. The father entertained their young son downstairs in our prayer room while I ministered deliverance to the son, through the mother, in my upstairs office. The child was set free from his autistic symptoms. The father later commented that he could see changes in his son happening before his eyes while I was still upstairs ministering through his mother. A couple of years later their son entered regular school without difficulty.

Another medically incurable disease is sickle cell anemia, a genetic disorder of the red blood cells. The red blood cells have an abnormal shape which can cause the cells to get trapped in the smaller blood vessels, causing pain and tissue damage. Children with parents whom can trace their roots to malaria laden areas, such as Africa or India, may be susceptible to this disorder. We had a black father come for prayer on behalf of his two small children, both of whom suffered with this disease. The Lord in His goodness healed them both.

There are exceptions to every rule, however, and we have on occasion ministered deliverance directly to a small child. One of our favorite stories is from a ministry session when the child was present. I had been a speaker at a Women's Aglow meeting in northern South Dakota one evening. Being

Ministering Deliverance to Children

located in a thinly populated area where the nearest baby sitter might live 30 or more miles away, this particular Women's Aglow chapter made several of their meetings open to entire families, husbands and children in addition to the ladies. After the meeting, a four year old pestered her parents to have us pray for her.

LeAnn had been a difficult child. She was adopted into a loving Christian family when about six months old, but resisted her parent's love and discipline and had become a rather unruly and disruptive child. Meals and bedtimes became traumatic family experiences. Even close relatives avoided being responsible for watching LeAnn as she was very difficult to control.

As we prayed for LeAnn, Doris saw a picture of how she had been treated and abused prior to being adopted. We took authority over some spirits such as rejection, fear, etc. as we ministered to LeAnn while being held in her mother's arms. We didn't see much in the way of a reaction to our ministry except a softening of her expression and a sense of peace as she chewed softly on one finger.

The following evening we were back in Rapid City and received a call from LeAnn's mother. She was so excited as the Lord had touched LeAnn in a wonderful way. She was much more at peace and others were even commenting on the changes in LeAnn. One key situation that had always been a difficult time had been bedtime. LeAnn usually resisted going to bed. After prayer, this changed dramatically and she was willing go to bed when it was time. We wonder if she hadn't been tormented by spirits at night and was now willing to go to bed because it was a peaceful experience. LeAnn soon became baptized in the Spirit as well and received a prayer language that she used. She also could sometimes be found sitting in the swing while she sang songs to Jesus.

Prayer for LeAnn took place over thirty years ago. The last we heard, she was a well-adjusted teenager. She was active in school athletics and cheerleading and remains a sincere Christian. This story is one of Doris' favorite stories: Jesus drew her, Jesus touched her, and Jesus continues to keep her.

As with adults, freedom from evil spirits is often a precursor to physical healing. We remember a little seven-year-old girl that was brought for physical healing by her mother and grandmother one evening. She suffered from multiple daily seizures. We ministered some deliverance as well as praying for healing. To our knowledge, she never had another seizure.

An interesting healing story happened one evening at a friend's house as we were closing our monthly officer's meeting for the local Full Gospel Businessmen's Fellowship. George was the local chapter president and his wife received a call from their daughter telling them that they had a sick granddaughter. The little girl had a temperature hovering around 104 degrees and they were concerned that they might need to take her to the emergency room at the hospital. They had called for prayer and so we officers gathered to pray for the little girl.

As we began to pray, it seemed as if I had the faith to believe that I could command the temperature to decrease by one degree to 103 degrees; so I did. We continued to pray and I thought that if I could command the temperature to decrease to 103 degrees, then I could command it to decrease another degree to 102 degrees; so I did that. We continued to pray and I continued to command the temperature to decrease by one degree at a time until we reached the normal body temperature of 98.6 degrees. Don't ask me why I didn't have the faith to command it to decrease all at once; I don't know. I just know that it seemed right (again, cooperating with God's Spirit), to walk the temperature down one degree at a time. I walked the 4 blocks home immediately after we finished praying. As I entered my house, George and Doris were talking on the phone. George was rejoicing that he had already heard from his daughter that his granddaughter's temperature had returned to normal.

In the above instance, it is easy to apply our principle of someone with spiritual authority over a small child requesting ministry for them, because the child was quite small and the mother called to ask for prayer. Sometimes the situations in which we find ourselves are not quite so well defined.

A case in point is one regarding a young man about twelve years old who had some learning disabilities. Normally we would not minister deliverance to someone as old as this without his express consent and only if he were present. The Lord led us differently in this particular situation.

This young man consistently found school to be quite difficult and discussions between the school authorities and his parents about placing their son in special education classes had occurred from time to time. Both go along. As we expel demons, the remaining evil spirits seem to weaken and are easier to cast out.

The end result is that the man is affected. The scripture passage quoted above indicates that "the last state of that man becomes worse than the first." We do not want our dwellings to be occupied by any other spirit than the Holy Spirit; and if it is, we place ourselves in danger of having problems!

Practical Applications

Be aware that evil spirits may seek certain physical locations from which to operate. They may feel more comfortable in familiar locations where they believe they won't be noticed and expelled. Spirits of sickness or death may congregate in a hospital awaiting an opportunity to invade someone's life. Sexual spirits may frequent areas of town where sexual activity is on-going such as motels or locations where prostitutes gather to ply their trade. We are not to be afraid, just aware, so we are not taken by surprise by the enemy.

Sometimes it is obvious that a home or place needs cleansing. If there is a lack of peace in a home, it may be caused by a resident spirit of conflict or unrest. Adverse supernatural activities, such as doors banging or pictures moving, indicate a need for cleansing of the premises. We once talked to a lady that had literally been tossed from her bed in the middle of the night. Christians do not have to put up with this sort of nonsense but many are unaware that they can exercise Christ's authority in this arena.

We recommend that cleansing of a home or dwelling occur when:

You move into a new home. It is never possible to know with certainty all the previous activities that may give spirits the right to inhabit a home.

Residing in a strange place where improper activities may have occurred. When staying overnight in a hotel or motel room, for example, I normally assume that the room needs to be cleansed and dedicated to the Lord's activities and presence, even if only staying overnight.

Occupying a new office. The Holy Spirit reveals the presence of a spirit that needs to be expelled. Keep alert, and the Lord will identify the enemy.

Cleansing is done by following the biblical examples discussed previously. First, remove any items that attract evil or give evil spirits an invitation to occupy your space. Books that promote witchcraft, Ouija boards, idols from foreign countries that carry a curse, etc. all need to be removed from the location in question. Next, a verbal pronouncement of dedication of the place to the Lord and His purposes is made. It is important that this commitment is verbalized as spirits are not able to know your thoughts, and the verbal announcement declares which side you are serving. Command any evil spirits present to leave. Normally, this is sufficient but on occasion the Holy Spirit reveals a specific name of a spirit that needs to be commanded to leave. Afterwards, honor the Lord in the place that has been cleansed. Fill the home with objects and activities that glorify God. Even the atmosphere can glorify the Lord by playing praise and worship music. Protection is maintained by staying alert to any enemy activity and exercising the Christian's spiritual authority to deal with any evil influence.

Some Personal Experiences

Over the years, we have prayed through several homes, motel rooms, and other places often at the request of someone who is experiencing some sort of supernatural difficulty. It is not unusual for the Holy Spirit to reveal the presence of some sort of evil spirit in these situations.

One of my first experiences with the need for cleansing a room or building was with a new Christian that had just come to the Lord. She called me because something wasn't right in the home she was living. Upon entering her bedroom in her house, it was almost as if I could feel the temperature drop. An evil presence was in that bedroom. It turned out that this young woman was involved in an out-of-wedlock sexual relationship that had given this spirit access into her home and, more specifically, into her bedroom. Repentance and cleansing occurred, and the situation ended happily as the changes in her life became a drawing card for her partner. He too soon committed his life to the Lord.

About the Author

Dr. Harms has earned B.S., M.S., and Ph.D. degrees in Civil Engineering. He taught engineering at the university level for eighteen years, rising to the tenured rank of Professor of Civil Engineering prior to becoming a water treatment process engineer with an international engineering firm. His consulting work took him from Maine to California and from Washington State to Florida in the U.S. and included several overseas assignments in Korea, Vietnam, and Indonesia.

The Lord interrupted his life in a powerful way while teaching at Virginia Polytechnic Institute and State University in 1974. He experienced the baptism with the Holy Spirit while a member of a Lutheran church and began ministering to the sick and emotionally troubled. He and Doris, his wife of over fifty years, have ministered in several locations in the U.S. as well as several countries in Europe and Asia. Lee and Doris have over thirty-five years experience in the healing and deliverance ministry. They are still actively involved in both. They regularly teach and equip others interested in these aspects of Christ's work.

If you have any questions or comments on the material in this book, they may be contacted using the information listed below.

Heartland Healing Rooms
P. O. Box 703
Raymore, MO 64083

Phone: 816-331-8023
www.heartlandhealingrooms.org

This book was prepared for printing by

King of Glory Printing & Publishing

Our goal is to help unpublished authors facilitate printing of their manuscripts in a professional and economical way. If you have a manuscript you would like to have printed, contact us:

336-818-1210
or
828-320-3502

PO BOX 903
Moravian Falls, NC 28654

www.kingofgloryministries.org